T0327923

The Royal Palaces

Secrets and Scandals

Quarto

First published in 2024 by Frances Lincoln,
an imprint of The Quarto Group.
One Triptych Place, London, SE1 9SH,
United Kingdom
T (0)20 7700 9000
www.Quarto.com

A catalogue record for this book is available from the British Library.

ISBN 978-0-7112-6939-2
Ebook ISBN 978-0-7112-6941-5

10 9 8 7 6 5 4 3 2 1

Design by Glenn Howard

Publisher: Philip Cooper
Senior Editor: Laura Bulbeck
Deputy Art Director: Isabel Eeles
Senior Production Controller: Eliza Walsh

Printed in Bosnia and Herzegovina

The Royal Palaces

Secrets and Scandals

Kate Williams

Illustrations by James Oses

Contents

Palaces are where monarchs planned battles ... gained their thrones, lost them, married, had children, were sentenced to death, survived murderous plots and kidnappings and even came close to murder themselves.

Introduction

Mary Queen of Scots returned from France to Holyroodhouse, after her husband, the King of France, died, leaving her a widow at eighteen. The young Queen filled the palace with boatloads of tapestries, decorations and furniture from France and it became a vivid, vibrant court once more. But she was always in danger, from men who wanted her power. On 9 May 1566, she was dining at Holyroodhouse with friends and her secretary, David Rizzio, when an army of nobles burst in, seized Rizzio, threatened her with a gun and dragged him downstairs to stab him. Her husband, Lord Darnley, had been among them. Mary was swiftly put under house arrest. She was pregnant and so the nobles could depose her for her son. It was the beginning of a bloody battle for power and it had taken place in Mary's own personal rooms. A monarch was never safe, not even in their own palace.

...

A palace is both a home and the headquarters of monarchy; it is where monarchs planned battles, even engaged in them, gained their thrones, lost them,married, had children, were sentenced to death, survived murderous plots and kidnappings and even came close to murder themselves. Charles I was executed, Henry VIII planned the end of some of his wives and secretly married Anne Boleyn, Edward VIII abdicated, James II was accused of smuggling in a fake baby during his wife's labour and promptly thrown off the throne, Owain Glyndŵr led rebellions against English rule, Conwy Castle became a Civil War stronghold, Windsor Castle was taken over by Oliver Cromwell, Charles II celebrated with endless revels, baby James VI was christened in a multi-million pound christening, and Elizabeth II took refuge as a princess during the Second World War – all of these events took place in the royal palaces.

From the earliest of times, chiefs or leaders of tribes and groupings would build themselves a fort or a larger residence, to signify their power and wealth. A monarch is denoted by a crown but he or she is also signified by their fort, castle or palace. Usually higher up and always larger than surrounding buildings, the palace was from the earliest times the monarch's fortress, from which their position was defended. And monarchs who were fighting to control land built forts in areas of rebellion and discontent, such as William the Conqueror ordering forts across England, including the Tower of London, and Edward I commissioning castles to attempt to control the Welsh. And later, in constitutional times, the palace was a building that was used to symbolise a country's power and history, particularly to representatives of visiting states, examples of wealth or sophistication meant to impress peers and public alike.

Monarchs also commissioned or bought new palaces, if they did not like the existing structure or its location, such as William and Mary looking for a property in the then country air of Kensington, George III buying his wife Buckingham House as a quiet retreat which turned into a giant palace. Or, as with Henry VIII and Whitehall with Anne Boleyn, perhaps it was because he had a new wife; or perhaps the rulers wanted a holiday palace, like Victoria and Albert purchasing Osborne House on the Isle of Wight or Balmoral in Scotland. And other palaces away from the bustling court of the main residence could be used to keep secrets, with mistresses given rooms in smaller palaces and Kew Palace used as a prison and asylum for George III when he was overwhelmed by mental illness. And when Mary, Queen of Scots was thrown from her throne, she was taken to Lochleven Castle, where she could be entirely isolated, and there she was forced to abdicate. And Diana, Princess of Wales used the privacy of Kensington Palace to make recordings for a journalist for the bombshell book that would ensure the end of her marriage.

Palaces are full of stories, and stories of what might have been. Linlithgow, one of the most beautiful ruined buildings in the world, was a stopping point for Bonnie Prince Charlie as he attempted to gain the throne his father had been denied. Princess Charlotte, the only legitimate granddaughter of George III, died after childbirth at Claremont House; her uncles rushed to marry and provide heirs, and thus Queen Victoria was born. Lady Jane Grey was installed as the nine-day queen, against her will, and her execution became inevitable. Edward VI was nearly kidnapped and died young, leaving the succession in the hands of his sisters, whom Henry VIII had not wanted. And Elizabeth I, who had narrowly avoided being accused of treason at the Tower, returned in triumph, to occupy her rooms before her Coronation, the same rooms that her mother, Anne Boleyn, had inhabited before she was executed.

A monarch is denoted by a crown but he or she is also signified by their fort, castle or palace. Usually higher up and always larger than surrounding buildings, the palace was from the earliest times the monarch's fortress.

Princess Diana chose a hospital for the birth of her children and royals are no longer born in palaces these days. But they are still married there, and most of all, they die there. To be a royal is to know the place in which you will die. Elizabeth II died in Balmoral, working until the end, and then was taken to Windsor, where she was buried with her parents, sister and husband.

Henry VIII most expanded the panoply of palaces, after taking church and monastic lands, as well as Cardinal Wolsey's Hampton Court Palace and Whitehall Palace. For Henry, the monarch's houses had to be the most magnificent and most numerous, and land was taken from both the rich and the poor. The landscapes of these islands have been shaped, figuratively, literally, politically, through the handful of dynasties who have controlled power for centuries. To be able to own, seize or control the land needed for a stronghold was rare enough. To then design, pay for, construct, maintain and defend a significant building was another thing. Some palaces have been lost, reminding us that power is always fleeting. Richmond and Greenwich, once great Tudor palaces, are no more. Whitehall once dominated central London until a fire in 1698. One of the defining characteristics of a palace or castle is that it is sturdy, and represents an investment of time, money and resources. So it is no wonder that many have been restored, rebuilt, redesigned and repurposed over the years and they are some of the most important buildings remaining from their period of time.

> *Palaces are full of stories, and stories of what might have been ... They were intended for a range of purposes, but they all have one thing in common. They were part of the story of the monarchy and of the countries of this island.*

'Life in a palace rather resembles camping in a museum', said the governess of Princess Elizabeth, future Queen Elizabeth II, about Buckingham Palace, which she thought 'dropping to bits'. Royals cannot sell a palace and swap it for a new one, they must live in the same place as their ancestors, work in the rooms that the former king or queen died, sleep in the same bedroom as their forebears. As a historian, I find the ins and outs of the construction, destruction, reconstruction and repurposing of these magnificent buildings fascinating, and I hope you will too.

In researching this book I have revisited all of the buildings included (a few no longer exist or are not open to the public), and they have opened anew my eyes to the significance and importance of such structures. Some are ruins, maintained by hardy volunteers, some are owned by the families. Many are now owned by the nation, and are safeguarded by wonderful institutions such as Historic Royal Palaces, Cadw and English Heritage, the National Trust, Historic Environment Scotland and visits to royal palaces administered by the Royal Collections. Some are still working or living buildings, even though they were designed and built for a different age. They were intended for a range of purposes, but they all have one thing in common. They were part of the story of the monarchy and of the countries of this island.

I dedicate my work on this book to the legions of people who endeavour to keep these prominent examples of our complex and fascinating history still standing.

Buckingham Palace

Buckingham Palace has hosted many famous people and heads of state. The gardens are where the queen held her many garden parties and staff have served hundreds of thousands of cups of tea.

Buckingham Palace

'A few hours ago I discharged my last duty as King and Emperor, and now that I have been succeeded by my brother, the Duke of York, my first words must be to declare my allegiance to him. This I do with all my heart.' So spoke Edward VIII in his final speech to the nation, in December 1936, no longer king. The Duke of York, his wife and two daughters, Princess Elizabeth and Princess Margaret, were pitched into a new life that they had never expected.

Earlier on that day, Princess Elizabeth and her sister were at their family home, 145 Piccadilly: a grand house with a ballroom and lift, dozens of rooms and a servants' floor – but modest by royal standards. The princess was writing up her notes from her swimming lesson when she heard shouts outside. She asked a member of staff why people were being so loud, and he told her that her uncle had abdicated and her father was now king. So her sister asked, 'Does that mean you're going to be queen now?' When Elizabeth replied yes, Margaret said 'Poor you'. Elizabeth continued writing up her notes from her lesson – but she added 'Abdication Day' at the top and underlined it.

Early in 1937, the family left Piccadilly for good to live in Buckingham Palace, which looks magnificent but was hardly a family home. It has 775 rooms, including over 180 bedrooms for staff, 19 state rooms, 52 bedrooms for royals and guests, and 78 bathrooms, as well as 92 offices, a swimming pool, a jeweller, a post office, a cashpoint, a squash court and huge reception rooms. The royals live in the North Wing; Elizabeth and Margaret had their own floor, with their governess, and saw their parents much less frequently. During the Second World War, the girls were sent to Windsor Castle. The palace was bombed nine times and a policeman was killed. On Victory in Europe Day, 8 May 1945, the girls, then 19 and 14, asked their father the king if they might go out with the crowds. The famously protective king allowed them out. As he said: 'Poor darlings, they have never had any fun.' Elizabeth and Margaret headed out into the crowds celebrating the end of the war, accompanied by some staff and some guards officers who were their friends. Elizabeth wore her army uniform of the ATS (Auxiliary Territorial Service) – she tried to pull down her

On Victory in Europe Day, 8 May 1945, the girls ... asked their father the king if they might go out with the crowds. The famously protective king allowed them out. As he said: 'Poor darlings, they have never had any fun.'

cap to disguise herself but one of the officers told her she should not do that to the uniform. They danced in the streets and also did the conga with the crowds – a chain of them even went in and out of the Ritz hotel. They gathered on Pall Mall and shouted, 'We want the king'. As the queen herself later recalled: 'I remember lines of unknown people linking arms and walking down Whitehall, and all of us were swept along by tides of happiness and relief.' They later appeared on the balcony themselves, with their parents and Winston Churchill.

Buckingham Palace was bought in 1761 by George III for Queen Charlotte – as a retreat for her – and he called it the Queen's House. A previous house on the spot might have been owned by William Blake, and later extended and then bought by John Sheffield, who became Duke of Buckingham. His illegitimate son sold it to the king. Queen Charlotte gave birth to nearly all of her 15 children in the palace and she was fond of it – but St James's Palace was the main royal residence. The queen turned the part of the garden normally used for vegetables into a menagerie – there was an elephant and a zebra and also monkey houses.

When George IV took over, he planned to renovate it and live at Carlton House, but the latter simply was too small. He threw a giant party there for gaining his regency in 1811, which was such a crush that dozens of pairs of shoes were found and some women lost their gowns. Rivers of wine were meant to run down, along the centre of the tables, with gold and silver fish swimming in them – but unfortunately, everyone only managed to sit down hours after the planned start time, and all the fish were dead. By the time George became king, Carlton House was insufficient for his needs. As one visitor in the 1825 *Tour of a Foreigner in England* declared: '[although] the royal or government palaces are among the

Princess Elizabeth (the future Elizabeth II) on VE Day

most remarkable in London, they serve to show how little the dignity of the sovereign is respected in England in comparison with other countries of Europe. To say nothing of St James's Palace (which the present sovereign has not thought fit for his residence) there are in Paris many hotels preferable to Carlton House.'

George IV decided to create a large palace out of Buckingham House, with his architect John Nash. The king was given £150,000 by Parliament and he wanted instead nearly half a million. Nash added a new block to the west, facing the garden, and the state and semi-state rooms of the palace are very much as Nash designed them. The north and south wings of Buckingham House were demolished and rebuilt on a grand scale with a giant triumphal arch, Marble Arch, in the courtyard, in order to celebrate the British victories in the Napoleonic Wars. Nash also added the

Royal Mews, which house the royal carriages, including the Gold State Coach, commissioned by George III in 1762, and since used for coronations. Unfortunately, it is not pleasant to ride in – Victoria referred to its 'distressing oscillation' and William IV thought it was more uncomfortable than being at sea.

In October 1834, the Clerk of Works at the Houses of Parliament was told to get rid of the tally sticks: small wooden sticks that were used in accounting. He took the two cartloads down to be burned in the furnaces of the House of Lords. But those furnaces were supposed to be for the burning of coal, and the wood fire burned so high that it melted the copper flues and began a chimney fire. By the afternoon, there was a burning smell in the Lords and there was smoke in the air – but at 4 p.m. the labourers tasked with putting out the fire believed it was done and left for the pub. By 5 o'clock, the first flames were

creeping under the doors and at 6.30 p.m. a giant ball of flame burst into the House of Lords. By the evening, all of the Palace of Westminster was on fire, and spectators were crowded on the bridges and beside the Thames. A competition was opened for new designs for the replacement. The king, William IV, offered Buckingham Palace as the new Houses of Parliament, but the offer was declined – it would have been such a different plan for London.

Queen Victoria was the first monarch to use Buckingham Palace as a permanent residence. Prince Albert thought the palace was in a shocking state; he considered the drains to be particularly bad, and complained that the windows were never clean because one team of servants cleaned the outside and another cleaned the inside, and there was awful waste. He applied himself to the renovation and the reorganisation of the interiors. But the palace was almost impossible to manage. In 1838, not long after the queen had arrived, a teenage boy, Edward Jones, broke into the palace and was found pretending to be a chimney sweep – he had stolen some of the queen's clothes, along with various objects including a regimental sword. He broke in again two years later and changed his mind – but after a few days, he was back. The queen had recently had her first child and her maternity nurse found Jones under a chair in the monarch's sitting room at midnight. He claimed that he had hidden under a servant's bed, helped himself to soup and various foodstuffs from the 'cook's kitchen', sat upon the throne, saw the queen and heard the princess royal (to use his own word) 'squall'. He was sent to the house of correction for three months. Less than two weeks after he was released, Jones tried to get back into the palace again. He was found, but not before he had taken meat and potatoes from the queen's pantry. He was again sent to the house of correction – and was again found hanging around Buckingham Palace on his release. He eventually went to sea as a sailor and lived in Australia.

Significant renovations were made to the palace in the reign of Queen Victoria, chiefly the completion of the East Front – the famous front façade, with its balcony. The family felt there were insufficient bedrooms for them, their attendants and guests, and so they sold Brighton Pavilion and used the money to create a new fourth wing – on the site of George's beloved Marble Arch, which was moved to Hyde Park, where it still stands today. By the reign of George V, the East Front was decayed, as it was made of soft stone, and so it was replaced with Portland stone. After Albert died, Victoria used the palace little, but it was enshrined as the working office and home of the monarchy. It perhaps reached its zenith under Elizabeth II, who hosted regular state visits and thousands of people for garden parties. More recently, the

palace saw a giant corgi and a bone in a light show suspended over it during the Platinum Jubilee, as well as concerts and the Cambridges driving away down the Mall after their wedding reception at the palace.

The famous gates, made in Bromsgrove, were added in 1911. Also built that year was the Mall, a ceremonial route to the gates of the palace from Admiralty Arch, past St James's Park and onwards to the Victoria Memorial. Designed by Sir Aston Webb, it was a tribute to Queen Victoria. It is a public road but it is closed for state occasions, such as Trooping the Colour, fly-pasts, concerts and also state visits, when it is used by the motorcades of visiting heads of state. The railings bore the announcement of Prince Charles's birth at Buckingham Palace in 1948. The enthusiastic crowds had been dispersed after the happy event so that the princess could get some sleep, and they returned to sing and cheer the next morning. Elizabeth was the first royal since the seventeenth century not to have her child's birth witnessed by politicians. The practice had been brought in after the birth of Mary of Modena's son, in St James's Palace, who was then declared to have been smuggled in via a warming pan. Queen Victoria's births were witnessed by politicians who, she complained, were only separated from her by a screen. By the early twentieth century, the politicians would wait in another room. Princess Elizabeth's own birth, occurring close to the General Strike, meant that the Home Secretary had to leave important discussions to assent to her legitimacy. By the time that Princess Elizabeth was due to give birth, her father, King George VI, decided it would be undignified to have all the prime ministers of the Empire waiting near his daughter's room – and abolished the custom.

In 1982, a policeman patrolling the grounds of Buckingham Palace noticed a half-drunk bottle of wine lying by the wall. A housemaid declared she had seen a man climbing up the drainpipe – the guards did not believe her. Thirty-two-year-old Michael Fagan had climbed up and was wandering around the palace, eating cheese and crackers and sitting on the thrones to see which one was softest. He also saw a room full of baby gifts for Princess Diana. He stole a bottle of Prince Charles's wine but said it was rather poor – 'cheap Californian' – and claimed he was looking for a toilet but only found bins full of 'Corgi food'. Alarms had been tripped but the police turned them off. Michael Fagan then wandered out of a back door and over a wall into the Mall, but not much later he returned, climbed over the wall, up a drainpipe and found his way to the queen's rooms. He had broken an ashtray on the way, so he arrived in the monarch's bedroom at 7.15 a.m. with a bleeding hand and a piece of glass. The queen rang her night bell, but no one heard it. She then tried to call the police via the palace switchboard, but no one arrived. Finally, she managed to find a housemaid, who called for help – and the duty footman and policeman duly arrived. Fagan said the queen did not speak to him, and instead rushed away to contact security; he was sent to a psychiatric hospital for three months. His mother said: 'He thinks so much of the queen. I can imagine him just wanting to simply talk and say hello and discuss his problems.' Fagan was also charged with stealing Prince Charles's wine – and acquitted in 14 minutes. The lack of security at the palace was a huge scandal. The Home Secretary, who had ultimate responsibility for the safety of the royal household, offered to resign but Margaret Thatcher, the prime minister at the time, would not allow it.

On 20 March 1974, Princess Anne and her husband, Mark Phillips, were returning from a charity ball to Buckingham Palace when a car forced them to stop. The driver, Ian Ball, jumped out and began firing a gun. Anne's protection officer, James Beaton, tried to intervene but his gun jammed and he was shot. Anne's driver, Alex Callendar, was also shot, as was a nearby journalist, Brian McConnell, who tried to help. Ball approached Anne and told her he was kidnapping her for a ransom of a few million pounds, which he would give to fund mental health services. He told her to get out of the car. 'Not bloody likely,' replied the princess. She later told the BBC: 'We had a discussion about where or where not we were going to go.' He told her that she had to go with him, and she refused but said she was 'scrupulously polite because I thought it was silly to be too rude at that stage'. Finally, Anne got out of the car with her lady-in-waiting and a passer-by, a former boxer, Ron Russell, punched Ball in the back of the head. A police officer was shot but another managed to arrest him. Ball was charged with attempted murder and kidnap, and detained under the Mental Health Act at Broadmoor. Inspector Beaton was awarded the George Cross; Callendar, McConnell and another policeman, as well as Russell, were given the Queen's Gallantry Medal. The queen also paid off Ron Russell's mortgage in gratitude.

Buckingham Palace is at times surprisingly exotic in terms of decoration. As Michelle Obama said, when she was invited for tea while on holiday in London: 'The queen showed us the gold room. There is a room full of gold. Everything in the palace was, like, "This is what we were trying to do in the White House."' When Victoria took up residence in Buckingham Palace, a large amount of decorative fittings from Brighton Pavilion were moved there, with some of the red and blue Chinese Luncheon Room made up of parts of the Brighton Pavilion's music rooms. Some of the palace is open to the public in the summer,

after it was initially opened in 1993 to fund the restoration of Windsor Castle.

The gardens of Buckingham Palace are its jewel, with over 1,000 trees, including over 80 different species of oak, and over 300 species of wild plants – and, with their 39 acres, they are the largest private gardens in London. When George IV remodelled the palace, he wanted a suitably grand private garden and he appointed William Townsend Aiton, who ran the Royal Botanic Gardens at Kew, to redesign the existing gardens. Aiton added the great lake, fed from the overflow of the Serpentine in Hyde Park, which once housed a flock of flamingos. He also added a Mound, an artificial bank to block the view of the palace from the Mews.

The garden dates back to James I, who bought some land close to Whitehall to grow mulberry trees for silkworms. Unfortunately, he chose the wrong type of tree and his plan failed. The palace gardens now contain over 40 varieties of mulberry trees, including one said to date back to the time of James I. Buckingham Palace has hosted many famous people and heads of state. The gardens are where the queen held her many garden parties and staff have served hundreds of thousands of cups of tea. For the queen's eightieth birthday, a party was held at the palace, attended by 2,000 children, chosen by ballot. The gardens were transformed into scenes from children's literature, including the Hundred Acre Wood. A play was performed in the gardens, and also shown on TV, in which villains stole the queen's handbag.

The queen's corgis famously ran behind her everywhere in the palace. Elizabeth's family had a corgi when she was a child and when she turned 18, she was given her own, Susan, as a present. Many of her subsequent corgis were bred from Susan. They had their own room in Buckingham Palace, where they slept on raised cushions and enjoyed freshly cooked food. Princess Diana called them the 'moving carpet' and they were often seen in official meetings. One group knocked over Diana's butler, Paul Burrell, and plenty of servants have complained about them yapping or barking. In 1999, one footman took his revenge and started adding gin to the corgis' bowls, thinking it was amusing to watch them drunk. But one corgi, 14-year-old Phoenix, died of alcohol poisoning, and the footman was in trouble.

In 2012, at the London Olympics, viewers saw Daniel Craig, as James Bond, visit the queen at Buckingham Palace, and then walk with her and her three corgis to a helicopter – from which she then appeared to jump and land in the Olympic Stadium. It was a moment that the 10-year-old in 1936 listening to the shouts outside her house, commemorating her father's accession to the throne, could never have imagined.

Whitehall Palace

TAXI

Whitehall Palace was destroyed by a great fire in 1698, but it was the most dazzling and beautiful of Henry VIII's palaces ... There are remnants of its old grandeur, including the majestic Banqueting House which still stands today.

Whitehall Palace

Early on a chill January morning in 1533, so early that the sun had not even risen, Whitehall Palace saw one of the most momentous weddings in royal history – and it was all a secret, attended only by the minimum of witnesses. Although the groom was a king, the celebrant was not the Archbishop of Canterbury but a clergyman whose name is not recorded, although most likely someone rewarded for assisting with the suppression of the monasteries. The wedding was shrouded in mystery. It is not even known whether it was the first marriage for the couple – it was likely they were married in even greater secrecy a few months previously. The bride was already pregnant. The wedding was a triumph for the couple – but they kept it to themselves. The king was prepared to risk sending the country to hell to gain his new wife.

On 25 January 1533, Henry VIII married Anne Boleyn at the Private Chapel in Whitehall Palace, after divorcing his first wife, Catherine of Aragon, and breaking from Rome in order to do so. For a man so fond of marrying, Henry, after Catherine of Aragon, went small on weddings. But the ceremony that mattered would be in Westminster Abbey, just over four months later, when a visibly pregnant Anne was crowned as Henry's queen. She travelled from Greenwich Palace to the Tower of London and then processed through the city in a 'rich chariot with cloth of silver' to the Abbey, where the ceremony took place, followed by a great banquet at Westminster Hall.

Whitehall Palace was destroyed by a great fire in 1698, but it was the most dazzling and beautiful of Henry VIII's palaces, with a sporting complex of courts for Henry's beloved real tennis, a tilt yard for jousting, a bowling green and a cockfighting pit (on the modern-day site of the Cabinet Office). Other than the majestic Banqueting House which still stands today, there are remnants of its old grandeur: a wine cellar used by Henry VIII, now under the Ministry of Defence building, and Mary II's steps, overlooking the River Thames. Anne Boleyn planned the renovations with Henry, but she did not get the chance to enjoy them for long. She was queen for just three years before she was executed on 19 May 1536. On the following day, Henry was betrothed to her successor – her former lady-in-waiting Jane Seymour. They married at Whitehall Palace only ten days later, on 30 May, in the Queen's Closet, which had been decorated for Anne. Henry's second queen had dreamt of renovating the apartments and living there forever, but the rooms were unfinished at her death and it was Anne's daughter, Elizabeth I, who would be the one to enjoy the palace and its fine gardens.

With over two thousand rooms at its peak, Whitehall Palace was the largest in Europe, a sumptuous Tudor palace likely to have looked very like Hampton Court, with elaborate fireplaces and windows. Whitehall had been a governmental space since the eleventh century, but the Palace became a grand residence in the reign of Henry VIII. Henry wanted a brand-new home there fit for a king. And he set his sights on the magnificent York Place in Whitehall, owned by his chancellor, Cardinal Wolsey. This had always been a private house, first built on lands owned by a goldsmith, and later owned by the Archbishop of York, hence the name York Place. York Place had been extended and renovated and under Wolsey's possession had become one of the greatest houses in London, full of lavish furniture and fittings, including cloths of silver and plates of gold. Henry took both Hampton Court and York Place from Wolsey, as the Cardinal fell from Henry's favour due to failing to get a divorce from Catherine of Aragon. Wolsey was sent to the Tower but he died on the way and thus avoided being executed. Delighted by his new palace taken from the man who was once his closest advisor, Henry found it most convenient – for he had not had a property in the centre of London and had been staying with the Archbishop of Canterbury when visiting Westminster.

The King and Anne had toured the house and dreamed of a great house and even made plans for renovating it over the Christmas of 1529, a year before Wolsey's death. It was to be their own new palace together, a grand residence for a new chapter in Henry's life. As illustrated by a conversation between two footmen watching Anne's coronation, in Shakespeare's *Henry VIII*, the change from York Place to Whitehall was confusing for many.

First Gentleman
Sir, you must no more call it York-Place,
that's past;
For, since the Cardinal fell, that title's lost:
'Tis now the King's, and call'd Whitehall.

Third Gentleman
I know it; but 'tis so lately alter'd,
that the old name
Is fresh about me.

Henry VIII died at Whitehall Palace in January 1547 and lay in state there.

He was succeeded by his three children in turn – Edward VI, Mary I and Elizabeth I – and when they lived at Whitehall, they like him, took the upper floors while the ministers occupied the lower floor. Mary I loved Whitehall and her wedding with Philip of Spain saw great jousting matches in the tilt yard. But it was under Elizabeth I that Whitehall grew to its true brilliance. The young queen loved the privy gardens, went out riding into St James's Park with Robert Dudley and enjoyed being so close to her ministers. She held masques and jousts, and loved to dance in the rooms. Elizabeth received the proposal of her final suitor, the Duke of Anjou, at Whitehall and a whole temporary banqueting house was erected in the grounds at over 300 foot in length and decorated with hundreds of lights, hung with exotic fruits, and with a ceiling painted with sun and stars. The delegates were hosted to what was described as the 'most sumptuous joust in history' – all celebrating the queen as the 'fortress of beautie'. She did not marry the duke, much to her advisors' despair.

Under James I, the palace flourished and became his near-constant seat. It saw many great masques and celebrations, and regular performances by Shakespeare's men. Inigo Jones designed the sets for some of the masques and later built a dedicated theatre in the palace. James commissioned a new, magnificent Banqueting House, for grand masques and receptions. The reign of his son, Charles I, saw yet more expansion of Whitehall and by the time it came to its end, the palace numbered 2,000 rooms – although it was somewhat haphazard, as courtiers built extra extensions onto their lodgings. Under James I, Henry VIII's cockfighting pit became a theatre and Charles I and later Charles II extended the theatre and used it for plays. The Cabinet Office still contains a reconstructed 'Cockpit Passage', a ghost of the days of court masques and celebrations.

Charles I commissioned Peter Paul Rubens to create murals for the ceiling, depicting James as justice, and bringing prosperity to both England and Scotland. These paintings compared the king to a god, and were dripping with the ideology of the divine right of monarchs. It was these murals that Charles I walked under and saw during his final journey from St James's Palace, where he had been kept to the spot that the scaffold for execution had been erected outside the Banqueting House. As he prepared to be executed in front of his own Palace on 30 January 1649, he gave a speech defending himself and the

Barbara, Countess of Castlemaine

rights of kings. 'I must tell you that their liberty and freedom consists in having government.' Adding: 'A subject and a sovereign are clean different things.' He then said: 'I am the martyr of the people.' But few heard his words, for the bitterly cold wind was blowing the wrong way. The executioner and his assistants wore wigs and masks so they would not be recognised. The block was usually high enough so that the person could kneel, but Charles's was so low that

The king was interested in science, and his patronage of scientific institutions is well documented. Less well known is his secret laboratory under his rooms.

he had to be nearly lying on the floor – he was told it could not be raised. After his death, the crowd came forward to dip handkerchiefs in his blood and cut off locks of hair. The king's head was stitched back onto his embalmed body and the corpse put on show in Whitehall to paying visitors (price of a ha'penny) for a week, before he was buried at Windsor.

When Charles II was restored to the throne in 1660, he took up residence in Whitehall Palace. He refitted the tennis court, used the palace as a route to swimming in the Thames and renovated the theatre with a new floor. He also moved in his mistresses, who had opulent homes there – most notably, Barbara, Countess of Castlemaine, one of Charles's most powerful mistresses who charmed the King, loved the entertainments at Whitehall and spent astronomical sums of money. On the very day Charles married Catherine of Braganza, Barbara staged her own protest: she put her lacy underwear outside her house for all to see – Samuel Pepys, who was passing by said 'it did me good to look upon them'. Barbara was making it clear who was boss. Catherine had no choice but to appoint her lady-in-waiting, and Barbara continued to dominate King and court. In the following year Barbara moved into the palace itself – triumph complete.

Charles II was the king who most believed in the power of the royals to heal through the ceremony of touching to cure disease, particularly scrofula. He touched thousands of ill people a year – reaching a total of almost 100,000 people over the course of his reign, or around 2 per cent of the population – usually at Banqueting House or the state apartments in Whitehall. After having their illness confirmed by a surgeon and promising that they had not been touched before, around 200 were admitted by token on Fridays, to be touched by the King.

In the Privy Garden, Charles built a giant sundial, adorned with portraits of the Stuart royal family, and used glass bowls to tell the time. He loved the sundial so much that a guard stood by it at all times. Then came renowned libertine, author of wild sexual poetry and courtier, John Wilmot, Earl of Rochester. Charles always let him off, despite the most shocking behaviour, including kidnapping a lady of the court who turned down his proposal of marriage, fighting drunkenly at court events and insulting Charles in his poetry. Samuel Pepys complained it was 'to the King's everlasting shame, to have so idle a rogue his companion'. Then in June 1675, after a dinner in the company of his friends and the king, Rochester ambled, while inebriated, into the Privy Garden and destroyed Charles's beloved sundial in a drunken frenzy, shouting: 'Kings and Kingdoms are overturned and so shalt thou.' The king was furious and Rochester had to flee Whitehall – a monarch who had overlooked so many offences was heartbroken about his sundial.

Charles II was interested in science, and his patronage of scientific institutions is well documented. Less well known is his secret laboratory under his rooms. Pepys once saw it and described it as 'the King's little laboratory under his closet, a pretty place, and there [I] saw a great many Chymicall glasses and things, but understood none of them'. The King was carrying out experiments – and he was also trying to cure diseases by using a very macabre recipe. He was fascinated by the medicinal properties of the human skull and he even bought a recipe for thousands of pounds to make a special medicine. The basic ingredients were: 5lb of human skull (of a person hanged or dead by some violent death), 2lb of hartshorn (antler of male red deer) and 2lb of ivory. These were minced, distilled, shaken, filtered and redistilled. The dose was seven drops, increasing by degrees up to 40 or 50 for pressing occasions such as stroke or lethargy (unresponsiveness). He called this concoction 'the King's Drops' and used it among members of his court against epilepsy, convulsions, diseases of the head, and often as an emergency treatment for the dying. It was even thought of as a truth drug. When he fell ill in 1685, he reached for his drops, but they did not work and he died in his rooms at Whitehall, begging on his deathbed 'not to let poor Nelly starve', referring to another of his mistresses, Nell Gwyn.

During the reign of William and Mary, a severe blaze broke out on 4 January 1698, after a maidservant left a candle unattended while drying sheets. The fire ran down to the Thames and obliterated the Palace and all its lodgings. The King ordered Sir Christopher Wren to save the Banqueting House. On the remains of Whitehall were built the offices of government. The greatest palace in the Tudor world burned to the ground and few in bustling Whitehall nowadays would even know it had been there.

Kensington Palace

Anne had an eye for design and architecture, and she completed the queen's apartments and created beautiful gardens at the palace.

Kensington Palace

Kensington Palace is one of the most famous royal palaces, epitomising seventeenth and eighteenth century grace and splendour and remembered by so many as the home of Diana, Princess of Wales and her sons.

When William and Mary took the throne in 1689, they felt that Whitehall Palace and its foggy Thameside air was unsuitable for the king, who had a weak chest. They searched for a house in a more rural part of London and hit upon a location in the pretty village of Kensington. They bought Nottingham House, as it was then called, from the Earl of Nottingham for £20,000 in the summer of 1689. It had first been built in 1605 and was rather small, so they immediately tasked Sir Christopher Wren with extending and renovating it – he didn't have long, as the court planned to move in for Christmas of the same year. Wren kept the initial building and added a pavilion at each corner. After the deaths of William and Mary, Mary's sister Anne took the throne and continued the renovations.

Anne had an eye for design and architecture, and she completed the queen's apartments and created beautiful gardens at the palace. Anne had married George, Prince of Denmark, when she was 18, at St James's Palace. He was a devoted husband. The pair suffered many miscarriages and stillbirths, and four children dead in infancy. One survived: the young William, Duke of Gloucester. He was beloved by the family and used to play soldiers with his uncle, King William, in the gallery of Kensington Palace. As he neared his eleventh birthday, the boy was given rooms in the palace and the royal family planned a grand celebration at Windsor Castle. After the party, he fell sick with a fever and headaches, and died within a week, much to Anne's terrible grief. The death of William also damaged Anne's relationship

with the king – he had loved the child and seen him as his heir.

In 1708, George of Denmark died at Kensington Palace. He had been a kind husband to Anne as a princess, and when she became queen, he had assumed a pioneering role. He had declared himself consort and subject, not king, even though as husband, he owned all her property and she was expected to submit to him. In the case of William and Mary, the main claim to the throne had been Mary's, and yet William (who did have a claim, but it was much weaker) had been determined to be king. George declared he would do as the queen commanded, and in not insisting on anything resembling a joint monarchy or any rights, he laid the basis for the model of the consort to the queen of Prince Albert and Prince Philip.

Anne was heartbroken to lose her husband. While she was weeping over him, Sarah, Duchess of Marlborough – once her best friend and advisor – arrived at Kensington without invitation and told her to leave the palace, and her husband's body, and go to St James's Palace. Anne did so, but she grew increasingly distressed with what she saw as Sarah's lack of sympathy over the next few days, and her insistence that the queen not indulge her grief. Anne had long tired of Sarah's high-handed ways, and was growing to prefer the gentle, calm company of Sarah's relation, Abigail Masham. In the months that followed, Sarah tried to gain control of Anne, but the queen pushed back – and finally, in April 1709, dismissed her forever.

After Anne died in 1714, George I took the throne and he renovated the royal apartments and created new state rooms. Architect and painter William Kent designed what became known as the Cupola Room to recall a four-sided cupola, or round dome, and painted the ceiling in gold and blue. The walls were brown and gold. The centre of the room displays the astonishing Musical Clock, on an ornate wooden pedestal, created over the last twenty years of his life by Charles Clay. Kent also decorated the superb King's Grand Staircase, which he painted with figures from the Court – including himself and the famous European phenomenon, Peter the Wild Boy, a child found living in the woods in Hanover in 1725 and brought to the court on the request of Queen Caroline.

After the death of Princess Charlotte of Wales in Claremont in 1817, the sons of George III, hitherto content with their mistresses, set off on a hunt to find wives. Between them, the 13 children of George III had managed only one legitimate child – Charlotte, daughter of the Prince Regent. There were plenty of illegitimate children; George III's third son, the Duke of Clarence, had 10 with the actress Dorothea Jordan. The fourth son, Edward, Duke of Kent, alighted on Victoire, widowed

Below Young Victoria

Princess of Leiningen. Her brother, Prince Leopold, widower of Princess Charlotte, persuaded Victoire to say yes. Less than six months after Charlotte's death, the Duke of Kent was married to Victoire in a joint wedding with the Duke of Clarence and his German bride, Adelaide. The duke and duchess were in Europe when Victoire fell pregnant – and the duke made the last-minute decision to race back to London for the child's birth, when his wife was eight months along. The baby girl was born on 24 May 1819 at Kensington Palace. The duke was jubilant, declaring her as 'plump as a partridge', although he noted she was more of a 'pocket Hercules than a pocket Venus'. He declared: 'My brothers are not so strong as I am; the throne will come to me and my children.' He was sure his daughter would one day take the throne.

The child was christened in the Cupola Room at Kensington Palace, but the Prince Regent – furious at the claims that this child would reign – refused the names his brother desired, including Charlotte and Georgiana. The child's first name was Alexandrina, for the Russian tsar, but she needed an English name. Finally, while the archbishop was waiting for a decision, the Prince Regent said she could take the name of her mother, Victoire, anglicised to Victoria. By calling her such a strange name, derived from the French (England's ultimate enemy, just a few years after the end of the Napoleonic Wars), he was signifying that she would never be queen. Victoria herself claimed happily that she was 'the first person ever to be called Victoria'. There actually had been others in the parish registers, but she was the first child of the elite to bear the name. Her father died not long after her birth and her mother wished to return to Germany but was dissuaded – the child had to be brought up in England.

Victoria's life in Kensington was isolated and lonely; she spent hours playing with her dolls and reading. The duchess hated George IV and William IV, and did everything she could to separate her daughter from them. Victoria was fond of her uncle Leopold, but he left to be king of Belgium in 1831. Her mother had fallen under the spell of John Conroy, who had been equerry to the Duke of Kent. Conroy was controlling and obsessed with money. He was convinced that Victoria would come to the throne as a minor, with the duchess appointed Regent, and he was set on being the power behind the throne.

Victoria was completely controlled under what Conroy called 'the Kensington System'. Her outings were restricted, she was constantly watched and she had to sleep in her mother's room. They wished to police everything – even her thoughts. As she grew closer to 18, Conroy and her mother realised it was possible that they would never gain power through a regency. The king, William IV, was set on living until Victoria reached her majority to thwart the duchess and Conroy. He had tried to give Victoria the income to set up her own household, but her mother had refused it. There had even been suggestions that Victoria should change her name to something more traditional, such as Charlotte or even Elizabeth, but the duchess vetoed it – they might have been trying to push her out of Victoria's life, but the name would always be a reminder of her position.

Victoire and Conroy took Victoria on tours around the country, infuriating the king, who saw them as royal processions. When 16-year-old Victoria fell desperately ill with typhoid while in Ramsgate, the duchess demanded that her daughter sign over privileges and appoint Conroy to her staff. Victoria refused and she never forgave her mother for trying to gain power over her when she was seriously unwell. The following two years saw her simply trying to survive. A grand eighteenth-birthday ball was thrown for her at Kensington Palace but the king did not attend. Finally, Victoria had reached her majority and less than a month after her birthday, her uncle died.

Victoria was woken early in the morning and went to her sitting room to be told by the Archbishop of Canterbury and Lord Conyngham that 'my poor Uncle, the King, was no more, and had expired at 12 minutes past 2 this morning, and consequently that *I am Queen*'. Her first act was to request an hour alone – which she had never before had. Then she removed her bed from her mother's room. She moved almost immediately to Buckingham Palace and left Kensington Palace forever.

Two of Victoria's daughters, Louise and Beatrice lived at the Palace and other minor royals lived there in the early twentieth century. During the Blitz, the Palace was hit and suffered extensive damage. After the war, Prince Philip stayed with his aunt while meeting up with the then Princess Elizabeth.

In 1960, after their wedding, Princess Margaret and Antony Armstrong-Jones, later created Earl of Snowdon, took up Apartment 1a in Kensington Palace. The Snowdons set about renovating their new home and, after three years of work, moved into the newly adapted rooms. The Snowdons lived at the Palace with their two children and threw parties and receptions for the fashionable and glamorous of London, with many invitees from the worlds of the arts.

In 1981, Apartments 8 and 9 were joined together to create a new home for the newly married Prince Charles and Diana, Princess of Wales. She had to find a way of cramming all their many wedding presents into the house – including a pair of Georgian chairs from the people of Bermuda, a large glass bowl from the Reagans and a diamond clock from Cartier. The renovations took time, and it was only just over a month before William was born that Diana and Charles could move in. She was delighted by William and Harry, whom she brought back to the palace after their births in hospital. The two princes were brought up at Kensington Palace and went to nearby nursery and junior schools.

In spring 1991, a young royal journalist was summoned to a working man's café in Ruislip, by a doctor he had met while covering Princess Diana's visit to the X-ray department of St Thomas' Hospital in London in 1986. The journalist, Andrew Morton, was doing some research for a biography of Diana – but the 30-year-old princess had her own ideas.

So, instead, Dr Colthurst acted as secret go-between. He set off on his bicycle as if he was paying a normal visit, carrying a tape recorder and a list of questions from Morton, and Diana talked and talked. 'I was at the end of my tether,' she said. 'I was desperate.' She even showed Colthurst love letters from Camilla to Charles. But it was all secret – so that Diana could deny meeting or knowing the journalist. After Morton's offices were burgled, files rifled and nothing stolen other than a camera, Diana grew worried that the Palace was aware that she had a contact. She had her sitting room at the palace swept for listening devices and shredded every piece of paper. When the book was written, Diana was given sections to read – usually by Colthurst, who would cycle to Kensington, or by Morton when she was meeting sympathetic friends.

Diana: Her True Story was published in June 1992 and serialised before publication in *The Sunday Times*. With the bombshell information that Diana had tried to commit suicide and her marriage had been in collapse, the country exploded. An MP suggested that Morton be put in the Tower. The Prince and Princess of Wales separated in December and the prime minister announced that Diana would live at Kensington Palace while Charles divided his time between Highgrove and Clarence House.

At the beginning of December 1995, the queen wrote to her son and daughter-in-law, pressing them to divorce. The divorce was finalised in May 1996. Just over a year later, Diana died in a car crash in Paris, chased by paparazzi until the end. In the week that followed, weeping members of the public left piles of flowers – in places five-feet deep – outside Kensington's gates. When Diana's body returned to London, she spent one night in Kensington Palace before travelling through the streets of the capital to Westminster Abbey, accompanied by Prince Charles, Prince Philip, Earl Spencer, and Princes William and Harry. As Alastair Campbell, government advisor and 'spin doctor', later said in his diaries, the

government and the Palace were concerned that Charles could be booed or even attacked by the crowd, but it was concluded he would be safe if accompanied by his sons. Diana had loved Kensington Palace and it was fitting that her last night was spent there.

After Diana's death, her apartment lay empty until it was turned into offices 10 years later. In 2013, the Duke and Duchess of Cambridge took Apartment 1a, Princess Margaret's former home, as their new property, after a multi-million-pound renovation. A four storey, twenty room apartment, the property has five reception rooms, and various bedrooms and staff bedrooms.

In the grounds of Kensington Palace is Nottingham Cottage. The cottage was designed by Sir Christopher Wren and has been used by various royals. In the words of Prince Harry, it's 'half a football pitch' from the main palace. In 1948, Marion Crawford, the devoted governess of the queen and Princess Margaret, retired there after working for the family since the girls were small. She was given the cottage for life, but the fallout after the publication of her memoir, *The Little Princesses*, meant she was forced to leave. She moved to Scotland, not far from Balmoral, where she always hoped to see the queen one more time. But she was never invited to the Castle.

Prince William lived at Nottingham Cottage with Kate from 2011 until moving to Apartment 1a in 2013. Prince Harry then took Nottingham Cottage, but he said it was rather small and he would often hit his head on the doorframes. As he wrote in his memoir, he went home in the evenings after work and would 'eat over the sink, then catch up on paperwork, *Friends* on low in the background' – and then he'd smoke a joint, 'trying to make sure that the smoke didn't waft into the garden of my neighbour, the Duke of Kent'. It was at Nottingham Cottage that he proposed to Meghan Markle, and the couple moved out after their marriage to settle in Frogmore Cottage.

Queen Mary encouraged the opening of Kensington Palace as a temporary home for the Museum of London from 1911 to 1914. In 1989, the charity Historic Royal Palaces took over running the Palace and undertook a multi-million -ound renovation on the State Rooms.

Kensington has had many famous residents, but for so many it will always be Diana's palace, bringing to mind those images of the flowers stacked up outside the gates in the week after she died.

Hampton Court

Hampton Court was the scene of Henry VIII's great triumph, when he achieved his dearest wish: a son ... There were bonfires and church bells, huge banquets across the country to celebrate.

Hampton Court

On All Saints' Day 1541, Henry VIII was praying in the Chapel Royal at Hampton Court when he was visited by a messenger with a letter. In the letter were the details about Catherine Howard's adultery. It was all theatre. Henry had arranged to be there so he could publicly receive the missive and thus condemn his fifth wife, who was then around 19 years old. He was 50, and they had been married for barely 18 months. The young queen was soon interviewed at Winchester Palace by Archbishop Cranmer and she was close to hysteria. Cranmer feared she might commit suicide. By the end of the month, she was sent to Syon Abbey under house arrest and forced to give up her wedding ring. Henry remained at Hampton Court. In early December, the men accused of adultery with the queen were hanged and she would be executed at the Tower in 1542 – after Henry introduced a special bill into Parliament stating that a queen had to acquaint the king with her previous sexual history after marriage, meaning that Catherine could be executed without the need for a trial.

Hampton Court was the scene of Henry VIII's great triumph, when he achieved his dearest wish: a son. The desire for a male heir was the reason why he had broken from Rome and ousted his two previous wives. On 12 October 1537, at 2 o'clock in the morning, Jane Seymour, Henry's third wife, gave birth to his only son, Edward. The king had hired hundreds of workers, who had to toil by candlelight, as he had set them the impossible task of completing a total renovation, in just five months, of rooms for the queen – in the shape of a womb – and new rooms for the baby. Edward was born there, much to the king's delight. At 47, he finally had a male heir. There were bonfires and church bells, huge banquets across the country to celebrate, and Henry sent gifts to 'all the estates and cities of the realm'.

The child was christened three days later, and Jane saw some of his wondrous christening procession, which the king had been long planning, from the baby's rooms to the Chapel Royal, with all the aristocrats, ministers and ambassadors in the newborn's train. Edward's half-sister, Elizabeth, bore his christening cloth and was herself transported by aristocrats. The font was on a structure so giant that it took up most of the Chapel Royal, and the baby was then taken back to Jane's rooms. But the queen was very ill. It had been a long and painful labour, and she was fading fast. She may have suffered an infection, or a blood clot, and she died at Hampton Court on 24 October, 12 days after she had given birth, aged probably 29. Henry was devastated by her loss. She had never been crowned, due to the plague, although Henry perhaps had been waiting until she gave birth to a boy. But she was the only one of his wives to receive a queen's funeral, at St George's Chapel, in Windsor. She was buried in the vault there, as was Henry when he died in 1547, 10 years after the birth of his longed-for son.

Henry VIII was the king who built and extended the most palaces in England, spending all the money in his coffers, as well as taking properties and money from his enemies and seizing religious lands and houses during the Dissolution of the Monasteries. When Cardinal Wolsey knew he was about to fall from favour, he gave Hampton Court to Henry, in 1529 but it was no good: he was still accused of treason and ordered to London. He died on the way and Henry was rid of the minister who had done so much for him. Henry had over 60 palaces, but Hampton Court was one of his favourites and he spent the equivalent of millions, in today's money, renovating it. Wolsey had himself taken Hampton Court from the Order of St John in 1514 and spent as much on it, aiming to create the grandest palace in England.

One of Henry VIII's first renovations was to extend the fabulous kitchens. His court was huge, at over one thousand people, and they needed to eat. He built the Great Hall and the Tennis Court. He also commissioned the splendid Astronomical Clock in the courtyard, 4½m (15ft) in diameter. The clock showed a wealth of information handy to the Tudor courtier – the date and time, number of days since the year had begun, phases of the moon, zodiac signs and the hour of high water at London Bridge – vital knowledge, for most courtiers and visitors travelled by barge and high water around London Bridge was dangerous and thus to be avoided.

Henry used Hampton Court rarely after the death of Jane Seymour, and Edward VI preferred Whitehall. Mary I, however, used it for her honeymoon with Philip of Spain and, in 1555, the court was called to Hampton Court to welcome the arrival of her baby; Elizabeth I also travelled there to witness the birth of the

child who would displace her in the succession. Mary's stomach was swollen, and she was deemed by her doctors to have all the symptoms of pregnancy. The child was thought to be due in April, but no baby came. The doctors suggested they had miscalculated and it was simply late. But in August, Philip returned to Spain. Mary was devastated. She believed herself to be pregnant again two years later, but by 1558, it was clear she was dying, and people switched loyalties to Elizabeth. Mary recognised Elizabeth as her heir on 6 November 1558; it was for her a final surrender. She died 11 days later at St James's Palace. Although she wished to be buried with her beloved mother, Catherine of Aragon, she was taken to Westminster Abbey and later shared a tomb with Elizabeth.

Elizabeth loved the space and the entertainment at Hampton Court. On 10 October 1562, four years after she had

come to the throne, she fell ill with what was thought to be a cold. Soon she was suffering from a fever and the doctors realised that the queen had smallpox. It was possible she could die – leaving the country without an heir. The queen recovered, with few scars, but Lady Mary Sidney who had nursed her had terrible scarring. Her husband declared that he had left her 'in mine eye at least the fairest' of ladies, and 'when I returned I found her as foul a lady as the smallpox could make her, which she did take by continual attendance of her majesty's most precious person'.

While Elizabeth was ill, she asked that Robert Dudley be made Protector of the Kingdom. As Dudley was tainted by suggestions he had killed his wife to marry the queen, ministers were terrified that Elizabeth would die, leaving him in charge, so there was much relief when she recovered. Dudley had many enemies and there was jealousy for his closeness to the queen. He was made a privy councillor.

When James I, son of Mary, Queen of Scots, came to the throne, he used the palace for entertainments and, in 1604, convened the Hampton Court Conference with members of the Church of England and representatives of the Puritan faith. But none of the inhabitants of the palace, from Henry VIII to James I, could have imagined what it would become in the reign of Charles I and the Civil War: his prison.

In 1646, Charles I was losing the war against the Parliamentarians. He fled Oxford disguised as a servant and managed to get north to the Scottish army. But in 1647, after much debate, they handed him over to the Parliamentarians. He was first imprisoned in Holdenby House, in Northamptonshire, before being transferred to Hampton Court. There, the army demanded the king accept their proposals, essentially giving Parliament much more power. He refused. He was well treated at Hampton Court and his children came to visit, and spent time running and playing in its garden in front of him, and he had his dogs, Gypsy the greyhound and Rogue the spaniel. He also had privacy to write letters and was allowed to keep his attendants. While there, he was painted by Peter Lely – a moment in time preserved of the king while he still lived, judged by an admirer of the artist as truly capturing the monarch's 'clouded majesty'.

The king began to fear that he was to be executed. In early November, at around 6 o'clock in the evening, Charles and three companions crept down the cellar stairs, into the garden and then to a boat on the river. Finally, one guard, thinking that they had not seen much of the king that day, directed another to open the doors. Charles's chamber was empty. He had left behind two letters. One was to the Parliamentarians, saying he had left Hampton Court in order to be heard with 'Freedom, Honour and Safety'. The second was to the guards, asking them to care for his beloved dogs, Gypsy and Rogue.

He had fled south, in the hope of boarding a boat to France. But there was no boat to be had and he travelled to the Isle of Wight, in the hope that the governor might be sympathetic. Instead, he was imprisoned in Carisbrooke Castle. Charles tried to escape again, but got stuck in the bars of his window. He was taken to be jailed in Windsor Castle at the end of 1648. Within a few months, he would die in front of Banqueting House.

The Parliamentarians sold off the contents of Hampton Court but largely left the buildings alone. When Charles II came to the throne, he preferred London palaces, as did his brother, and it wasn't until William and Mary came to the throne in 1689 that the palace was occupied once more. They considered knocking it down and rebuilding it, but fortunately decided that would be too expensive, so kept half of the Tudor sections, building on their own extensions in seventeenth-century style, with staterooms and receiving rooms for the king and queen, and reception rooms overlooking the Privy Garden. Mary died in 1694, only five years after coming to the throne, at Kensington Palace, and William lived rather sadly at Hampton Court. He had the famous maze planted in 1696 and died after falling off his horse in the park in 1702.

George II was the last monarch to reside at Hampton Court, and under Queen Victoria it was opened to the public. It became a huge hit and a railway station next door to the palace was opened in 1849, for the floods of Victorian tourists keen to see where Henry VIII's court had feasted, celebrated and, for many, been sentenced to die. It is now managed by Historic Royal Palaces and open to the public all year round.

Palace of Holyroodhouse

In the nineteenth century, staff at Holyrood ran a flourishing side hustle, charging visitors money to see Rizzio's bloodstains in the queen's chamber.

Palace of Holyroodhouse

On the evening of Saturday, 9 March 1566, Mary, Queen of Scots was dining in her private rooms at her home of Holyroodhouse in Edinburgh, with friends and her secretary, David Rizzio. Her husband, Lord Darnley, was out, presumably in the taverns of Edinburgh. She was six months pregnant but had already grown weary of her husband, whom she had married the year before in her private chapel at the palace. He demanded power and was constantly plotting with his family against her; as Thomas Randolph said, she 'repententh her marriage' and was wary of his family. Darnley had offended the lords who controlled power in Scotland, especially Mary's half-brother, James Stuart. But then, he turned coat and decided to ally with them in a power grab against Mary. Now that she was pregnant, she could be deposed for the child and Darnley could be Regent. They would capture Mary – and the excuse would be David Rizzio, her secretary, who was Catholic and thus blamed for attempting to restore Catholicism and even accused of being Mary's lover. Darnley and a large group of lords broke into Mary's closet at about 8 p.m. and demanded she give up Rizzio. She refused and tried to shield him, but he was seized and one of the lords terrified her by waving a gun at her pregnant stomach. Rizzio was hauled through the bedchamber, stabbed and thrown down the staircase. He was stabbed 57 times, and the lords insisted that Darnley plunge the final knife in.

Mary was imprisoned. But she brilliantly won over Darnley, telling him that they were both in danger, and they escaped. She later returned with her supporters to Edinburgh – the rightful queen. In June, she gave birth to her son, James, an heir, at Edinburgh Castle. IThe arrival of a son sealed her doom, for now she could be thrown off her throne in favour of baby James. In 1567, early in the morning

Top David Rizzio
Middle Lord Darnley
Bottom Mary, Queen of Scots

of 10 February, a cataclysmic explosion shook Edinburgh. Lord Darnley had been staying in a house near the city walls, and Mary had visited him and then returned to Holyroodhouse for the wedding of one of her servants. The terrible explosion of gunpowder blew up Darnley's house and he was found in the nearby orchard – his valet dead next to him – with a chair, a rope, a dagger and two dressing gowns. He had heard the intruders, tried to escape but the killers found him and smothered him.

In the nineteenth century, staff at Holyrood ran a flourishing side hustle, charging visitors money to see Rizzio's bloodstains in the queen's chamber. It was, in truth, made with cochineal dye, but those who saw it got a thrill.

The magnificent Holyroodhouse dates back to the time of James IV, who built it at the beginning of the sixteenth century, next to the

Abbey that had been standing since the early twelfth century. James IV built a grand palace in Gothic style and James V, the father of Mary, Queen of Scots, extended it. It became the main seat of the court. Mary was sent to France aged five and returned to Scotland when she was 18, with boats full of tapestries, furniture and books that she had purchased, and instituted a new court of beauty and elegance. Within six years, Mary had been forced to abdicate in favour of her son, with her half-brother as Regent. After a failed battle, she was brought back to Edinburgh and stayed in Holyroodhouse, before her captors realised that ordinary people were determined she should be their queen – and so they stowed her away in Lochleven Castle.

In 1603, Mary's son, James, was at Holyrood when he was informed that Elizabeth I had died and he was now king of England, Ireland and Wales, as well as Scotland. James spent his time in England, and Holyrood was silent; in the Civil War it was full of Cromwell's troops. When James II came to the throne, he was so hated that when his wife, Mary of Modena, bore a son, gossip had it that the baby had been smuggled into St James's Palace, where she gave birth. James and his family were exiled, but his son, the smuggled baby, and then his grandson, Charles Edward Stuart, were determined to regain the throne. In 1745, Charles Edward or 'Bonnie Prince Charlie' came to Scotland in an attempt to seize the throne and set up court in Holyrood. On 17 September, cheered by crowds 20,000 strong, who had gathered in the streets to see the prince, he strode into the palace, which by this point was run-down. Rebuilt as a palace in the 1670s, after it had burned down during the Civil War, the renovated palace had not yet been inhabited by a monarch. Bonnie Prince Charlie used the palace as his HQ, from where he planned to take England and rule as king. But he only ruled from there for six weeks. While heading south to capture the English throne, he was forced to retreat. He managed to escape the clutches of the English by dressing up as an Irish spinning maid named Betty Burke, and he eventually fled to France.

In the early nineteenth century, George IV visited Scotland, the first monarch to do so since Charles II. The festivities were orchestrated by Sir Walter Scott, chief Scotland romancer, and demanded that all attending the balls wear tartan, thus setting off a craze back in England. George had the palace renovated, but instructed that Mary, Queen of Scots' apartments should not be changed. George V, in the twentieth century, had the palace restored and a lift was added, and Queen Elizabeth II spent one week a year there at the beginning of her summer break. Holyroodhouse saw a woman pushed from the throne in violent ways, and then her very distant descendant, Elizabeth II, become the longest reigning queen in British history.

Beaumaris Castle

Beaumaris is a great example of a castle vital to the Welsh rebellion, but also one of the very few castles in Britain that was never finished.

Beaumaris Castle

In 1400, Owain Glyndŵr claimed his title of Prince of Wales and began a 15-year Welsh revolt against English rule. A descendant of Welsh royal families, Owain had fought under the English king in the army. But in his forties, he had been twice betrayed by the English system: over possession of land seized from him by Lord Grey, as well as being cast as a traitor for not supplying troops for the king's army – even though he had been given the command too late by Lord Grey, who then blocked Owain's letter defending himself. There was great dissatisfaction among the Welsh at English rule and unequal treatment. Owain led a rebellion against Henry IV, capturing English castles. In 1402, the English Parliament issued punitive laws against Welsh people, preventing them from bearing arms, occupying positions of senior public office and buying property in English towns, as well as forbidding assembly in public and attempting to restrict the education of Welsh children. This only prompted more Welsh people into joining Glyndŵr; also, Scotland, Brittany and France sent military and naval aid to assist the Welsh forces, which gained much of the country. In 1403, Owain's forces captured the castle of Beaumaris – a great triumph.

The castles that seem so beautiful to us today were symbols of oppression for the Welsh. Beaumaris, like Conwy Castle, was

There was great dissatisfaction among the Welsh at English rule and unequal treatment … The castles that seem so beautiful to us today were symbols of oppression for the Welsh.

Beaumaris was never finished despite the huge amount of resources and money already invested in it … The castle as we know it now, one of the most impressive of its time, still can only hint at what it might have been.

commissioned in the late thirteenth century by King Edward I of England, as part of his attempt to control North Wales, and was designed by James of St George. However, unlike the other castles of Edward's 'iron ring' – Conwy, Harlech and Caernarfon – Beaumaris was never finished despite the huge amount of resources and money already invested in it. The threat from Scotland had overtaken the threat from Wales, and rising costs and the depletion of the royal coffers meant that construction was stopped early, well before the outer defences and inner buildings had been completed. The site – named after the *beau marais*, or 'fair marsh', on which it was built – was not as strategically important as that of other nearby castles, and the aspirational design was considered too expensive to finish.

Although the building work had been halted by 1300, the English still saw North Wales as both a valuable asset and a tempting target, and over the next few decades, occasional attempts were made to repair crumbling stonework and complete the original design. These attempts were never to fully succeed and the castle as we know it now, while undeniably one of the most impressive of its time, still can only hint at what it might have been.

Yet, despite being unfinished, there was still much value in the existing structure. Its four layers of defensive walls meant it was capable of being held against a much larger force, and the inner buildings were useable enough to be pressed into service. Those involved in the Glyndŵr rebellion were determined to take it and did so. But although the revolt had great early success, it did not last. By 1409 much of Wales had been recaptured by the English. Glyndŵr came under siege at Harlech Castle and escaped disguised as an old man. He and his followers fled to the countryside and staged attacks on English forces – who could not capture them. Glyndŵr repeatedly refused pardons from King Henry V of England and, despite the large ransom on his head, was never betrayed. But his was the last Welsh rebellion.

Once Beaumaris was retaken by the English, it was manned for another two centuries, although in an increasing state of dilapidation. In the early seventeenth century it was deemed decayed beyond redemption, although it still became a flashpoint during the English Civil War, and changed hands between the Royalists and Parliamentarians on more than one occasion.

After the Restoration of King Charles II, Beaumaris appears to have been stripped of its valuables and left to the elements. It remained largely untouched and increasingly overgrown, until the Romantic renaissance and rise of tourism in the nineteenth century led to growing interest in the medieval history of North Wales. Before her ascension to the throne, the future Queen Victoria visited the ruins as part of the National Eisteddfod. Beaumaris is a great example of a castle vital to the Welsh rebellion, but also one of the very few castles in Britain that was never finished. Even medieval monarchs gave up on building works sometimes.

Owain Glyndŵr

Greenwich Palace

Greenwich Palace, or the Palace of Placentia, is no longer standing. It reached its apogee under the Tudors, and much of its area is covered now by the Royal Naval College.

Greenwich Palace

Greenwich Palace, or the Palace of Placentia, is no longer standing. It reached its apogee under the Tudors, and much of its area is covered now by the Royal Naval College. A large red-brick structure arranged around gardens and a tilt yard, set beside the Thames, Henry VIII and his daughter Elizabeth I loved the palace and spent much time there. The palace dated back to the mid-fifteenth century, built in the 1430s by Humphrey of Gloucester, who was Regent to the young Henry VI. But after the king came to his majority and married Margaret of Anjou in the following decade, Humphrey fell from grace: he was imprisoned for treason and died in prison. Queen Margaret, only 17, took over the palace and named it the Palace of Placentia. An adjoining friary and church were built later in the century, and used for royal christenings and marriages. Henry VIII was born there, as was his daughter with Catherine of Aragon, the future Mary I, and his daughter with Anne Boleyn, the future Elizabeth I.

The palace was also the scene of Anne Boleyn's downfall. At the beginning of 1536, that most fateful year, she miscarried and the child was rumoured to have been a boy. She had, it was said, miscarried her 'saviour'. She had had four pregnancies, and Elizabeth, born three years previously, was her only child. On the same day, 29 January 1536, Henry wore black for his first wife, who was being buried in Peterborough Cathedral – not as the former queen but as the former Princess of Wales, wife of Arthur; her marriage to Henry had been deemed void. Catherine had died earlier in the month, after living in miserable house arrest at Kimbolton Castle. Henry had promised she could have better quarters and would be allowed to see her daughter if she and Mary agreed to recognise Anne as queen, but they would not. When Catherine died, Anne Boleyn was suddenly extremely vulnerable. The former queen had protected her – Henry could never cast aside Anne while Catherine was still alive, for he would be expected to return to her. Anne was distressed by Henry's wandering eye and penchant for mistresses, and he was impatient with her jealousy and angry that she did not have a son. He had fallen in love with her lady-in-waiting, Jane Seymour – who had also been lady-in-waiting to Catherine – probably in the previous year. Jane's serene personality was a pleasant contrast to Anne's. By early 1536, Henry was devoted to Jane and had asked about the possibility of annulling his second marriage: Anne's days were numbered.

Greenwich's tilt yard was the jewel in its crown: the size of a large park and containing a five-storey tower for watching the jousts. Henry, a great jouster, used it to show his prowess.

Greenwich's tilt yard was the jewel in its crown: the size of a large park and containing a five-storey tower for watching the jousts. Henry, a great jouster, used it to show his prowess and Anne was often in the audience, cheering him on. On 24 January 1536, the 44-year-old king had a severe fall from his horse and it was thought a 'miracle that he was not killed'. Perhaps, as historians have argued, the severe smash affected his brain, or perhaps the brush with death and having to face up to ageing made him think he had little time left – he was without an heir, and his realm would be in chaos if he died without a son. The failure of Anne's pregnancy just a few days later confirmed his fears. He had come to think that God would not give him a son while he remained married to Anne, and that his marriage was in fact 'displeasing to God'. He was asking ministers how he could free himself from the union and Thomas Cromwell was deputised to investigate. Henry left for London for the Shrovetide celebrations in early February, leaving Anne alone. Ambassador Chapuys noted that 'he has left her in Greenwich, whereas formerly he could not leave her for an hour'.

By spring, the king and his advisors were preparing to prosecute Anne for adultery at trial. But there was scant actual evidence against her. Mark Smeaton, Anne's musician, was taken to Cromwell's house and interrogated, if not tortured (aristocratic gentlemen could not be tortured, whereas he could). On 1 May 1536, Henry VIII was holding the great May Day jousts at the tilt yard in

Greenwich Palace. He left abruptly, shocking the spectators, halfway through. Anne was left abandoned in the crowd – and she would never see her husband again. The king had been told by his minister, Thomas Cromwell, that a case for claiming the adultery, and thus treason, of Anne Boleyn was now advanced. A confession had been forced from Mark Smeaton and Cromwell had had other members of the queen's circle interrogated to back up claims of her adultery with various men, including her brother George Boleyn – which made her guilty of high treason. Using Smeaton's forced confession, Henry pressed the button for ridding himself of the wife he had fought so hard for and who had given him only a daughter.

Greenwich, which had been the site of much happiness for Anne, watching jousts and games with her husband, the king, had come to be the theatre for her end.

Anne's final entries in her household book include two leading reins with buttons and tassels for the little Princess Elizabeth, and her last entry on 28 April was for a cap of taffeta with a caul of gold.

On 2 May, Anne was watching a game of tennis. She was regretting not having bet on her champion, when she was told by a messenger to present herself to the Privy Council at Greenwich, in the Council Chamber. The king was in Westminster; she was told by three men – among them her uncle, the Duke of Norfolk – that she was guilty of 'evil behaviour', including adultery with Mark Smeaton, Henry Norris and others they did not name. Anne tried to defend herself, but they refused to listen. She was taken back to her apartments and given dinner, and then Norfolk, along with Thomas Cromwell and other men of power, came to her apartments with an arrest warrant.

Anne was taken to the barge for the journey to the Tower. Greenwich, which had been the site of much happiness for her, watching jousts and games with her husband, the king, had come to be the theatre for her end. It took her three hours to reach the Tower, where she would be accommodated in the rooms she had occupied before her magnificent coronation. She would be executed just over a fortnight later.

Henry VIII married Anne of Cleves at Placentia at the beginning of 1540 but was very dubious about her, and declared she was not so fair as she had been described. He had also seen her beautiful, young lady-in-waiting,

Catherine Howard, and grown infatuated. By July of the same year, Henry had annulled his marriage and Anne of Cleves had become his 'most beloved sister'; by the end of the month, he had married Catherine Howard.

Henry's much desired son, Edward VI, died at the age of 15 in the palace. He had never been strong, but in early 1553 he was very ill with a fever. When there was a recovery, he was moved to Greenwich with the court. In May, he was held up at the window to see three great ships set out onto the Thames, and everyone was to say the king was well. Three Londoners heard saying that he was dying had their ears cut off as a punishment. By June he was very sick: unable to sleep without opiates, and coughing up greenish-yellow and black mucus, with his face and legs very swollen. On 1 July, he was shown to the public outside his bedroom window, but he looked seriously unwell and people started to panic. He died five days later and his last words were: 'I am faint. Lord have mercy upon me and take my spirit.' There was no heir; Henry's long-fought-for son had died. The men around him decided Lady Jane Grey should be queen, the first woman to sit upon the English throne.

Lady Jane Grey was deposed by Mary I after nine days, but the latter ruled for only five years before she died. Elizabeth I then came to the throne, decking herself in Tudor propaganda as she was crowned. Elizabeth was not commonly at Greenwich Palace, preferring Richmond and Whitehall, perhaps because her mother had been so cruelly treated there. However, she kept up the palace's functions, including the superb royal armoury, which created an elaborate set of armour for her devoted companion, Robert Dudley.

In 1597, Elizabeth had been on the throne for 40 years and there had been various threats to her life. However, her ministers were endlessly frustrated by her refusal to admit the importance of most of the plots, from poisoned gloves to bombs. Indeed, some of them she never even knew about, they were so badly executed. In July 1597, Edward Squire, a Greenwich man, who was working in the queen's stables, put poison in her saddle – but the queen went out riding and the poison had no effect. It would have had to be an exceedingly powerful substance to penetrate the queen's thick riding outfit. She only found

By July of the same year, Henry had annulled his marriage and Anne of Cleves had become his 'most beloved sister'; by the end of the month, he had married Catherine Howard.

Edward Squire ... put poison in her saddle – but the queen went out riding and the poison had no effect. It would have had to be an exceedingly powerful substance to penetrate the queen's thick riding outfit.

out a year later, when a captured Catholic soldier revealed the plot, in an attempt to save his own skin. Squire was arrested and tortured; he admitted his guilt but cried that the queen had not been affected. He also claimed to have put the same poison on the Earl of Essex's chair. He was hanged, disembowelled and quartered at Tyburn for high treason. It is probable that Squire was set up – his accounts of the poison differed: in one he claimed a Jesuit, Richard Walpole, had written out a prescription for a 'poisonous confection' consisting of opium, white mercury and two powders, 'one yellowish and the other brownish'. In another account, he claimed that Walpole had already prepared the poison and given it to him 'in a double bladder, wrapped about with many parchment wrappers'. He was certainly a stooge, and an exceedingly hapless poisoner.

Under James I and Charles I, the Queen's House was built next to the main palace – a white stucco house unlike the rest of Placentia. Anne of Denmark, wife of James I, commissioned Inigo Jones to build her a beautiful house in which to display her artworks, and Henrietta Maria, wife of Charles I, asked Jones to complete it in 1635. The handsome Palladian gem was revolutionary for its classical style and much admired. When Mary II asked Christopher Wren to plan the Old Royal Naval College, she instructed him that the new building should not obstruct the view of the Thames from the Queen's House. The Queen's House is now owned by the National Maritime Museum in Greenwich and displays paintings from the Museum's collection.

In the Civil War, the palace became a barracks for Cromwell's soldiers, and although Charles II meant to rebuild it, he spent most of his time at Whitehall, and the King's House he also had built was never used. At the end of the seventeenth century, much of Placentia was demolished.

Queen Mary II, of William and Mary, had been distressed by the plight of wounded sailors and asked for the palace to be adapted as the Royal Hospital for Seamen, along the same lines as the Chelsea Hospital for soldiers. The Queen's House and the area around the site of the former Placentia were used in the 2012 London Olympics for equestrian events; the Tudor court would have approved.

Balmoral Castle

The queen's piper played under Victoria's window every morning when she was at Balmoral – a tradition that Elizabeth II continued.

Balmoral Castle

In the 1840s, Victoria and Albert were on the lookout for a castle they could call a family home. After a stay in Scotland, they became convinced that they had found the right place – Albert thought the countryside looked like that of his home of Coburg, and Victoria liked how far it was from the hustle and eyes of the press and court in London. They took the lease on Balmoral, sight unseen, and when they arrived for their first visit, although they were charmed they deemed it too small. They immediately began building extensions and further living quarters, and bought the house for £32,000 in 1852 (around £4 million now). Victoria covered it in tartan and thistles, an interior design choice that some visitors found baffling. 'The curtains, the furniture, the carpets, the furniture are all of the different plaids,' Secretary of State Lord Clarendon noted in 1856. 'And the thistles are in such abundance that they would rejoice the heart of a donkey if they happened to look like his favourite repast, which they don't.' Other guests were astounded by the freezing walks and the endless bagpipes: Victoria loved them, and the queen's piper played under her window every morning when she was at Balmoral – a tradition that Elizabeth II continued.

Balmoral allowed Victoria to be informal. After Albert died, leaving her a widow at the age of 42, with nine children, she withdrew from much of society, prompting calls for her to be seen – as if a queen did not exist if not seen. John Brown, seven years Victoria's junior, had worked on the estate since he was young. In 1851, Prince Albert gave him a permanent role and made him leader of the queen's pony. After her husband died, Victoria leaned more and more on John Brown, walking with him, riding with him and spending hours with him at Balmoral, much to the despair of her children and her ministers. They were terrified that he had power over her and might

influence her in terms of policy – and called her Mrs Brown, as they had once called her Mrs Melbourne, for being too influenced by her prime minister. Victoria was devoted to Brown – although she never thought of him as more than a faithful servant. But when he died, she was overwhelmed with grief, writing: 'Perhaps never in history was there so strong and true an attachment, so warm and loving a friendship between the sovereign and servant … Strength of character as well as power of frame – the most fearless uprightness, kindness, sense of justice, honesty, independence and unselfishness combined with a tender, warm heart … made him one of the most remarkable men.' As she said, comparing his death to that of Albert: 'Life for the second time is become most trying and sad to bear deprived of all she so needs.' She commissioned a handsome new statue of him, inscribed with 'Friend more than Servant', and put it in pride of place on the estate.

Queen Victoria decreed what would be in her coffin when she died – Albert's dressing gown and the cast of his hand, various other trinkets and mementoes, and a photo of John Brown, a lock of his hair and his mother's wedding ring. After she died, her children took revenge on her affection for the servant. Her daughter burned sections of the diaries and her son, the new king, Edward VII, destroyed many memorials of Brown at Balmoral. Although he didn't destroy the life-size statue of Brown that the queen had commissioned, he moved it to an obscure spot, signalling the end of John Brown's long tenure.

By the time of Queen Elizabeth II's reign, the Balmoral estate was 50,000 acres, with individual houses for other members of the royal family, including Birkhall, which she had used when she was a child, a handsome white house, built in 1715 and purchased by Victoria as it was part of the Balmoral estate. It was given by George V to Elizabeth's parents and her mother kept it until she died. Elizabeth was at Birkhall when the Second World War broke out. As Queen, Elizabeth enjoyed the informality of Balmoral. On one occasion, she met some American tourists, who asked where she lived and she said she had a holiday home over the hill. As Princess Eugenie said: 'I think Granny is the most happy there. I think she really, really loves the Highlands.' She added that there were 'walks, picnics, dogs – a lot of dogs, there's

Queen Victoria decreed what would be in her coffin when she died – Albert's dressing gown and the cast of his hand, various other trinkets and mementoes, and a photo of John Brown, a lock of his hair and his mother's wedding ring.

Mrs Thatcher once came and suggested she might do the dishes, but Elizabeth prevailed. David Cameron also tried to put on rubber gloves and help with the washing-up.

always dogs'. The queen spent every summer break at Balmoral and prime ministers came up to visit her there. There would be outdoor barbecues where the Duke of Edinburgh cooked the sausages, and the queen collected the plates and did the washing-up. Famously, Mrs Thatcher once came and suggested she might do the dishes, but Elizabeth prevailed. David Cameron also tried to put on rubber gloves and help with the washing-up, and heard the queen say, 'What on earth is the Prime Minister doing?' He sat down again quickly. Tony Blair called the castle a 'mixture of the intriguing, the surreal and the utterly freaky'.

Princess Diana's second part of her honeymoon was spent at Balmoral – it was not the young bride's idea of a dream holiday. The honeymoon was a disaster: Diana found the routine oppressive and Charles left her alone to pursue his interests. It was a firm signal that she was expected above all to fit in and do what the royals had always done. Diana disliked Balmoral and loved escaping to go to London. 'I panic a lot when I go up to Balmoral. It's my worst time, and I think: "How the hell am I going to get out of this?" The first couple of days I'm frightfully chirpy when I get up there and everything's wonderful,' Diana said. 'By the third day they're sapping me again. There are so many negative atmospheres. That house sucks one dry.' The young princes, William and Harry, loved Balmoral, where they learned to fish and spent time running outside with their cousins. It was there, during their summer holiday in 1997, that they learned that their mother had been killed in a car crash in Paris. Harry remembered his father coming to give him the news, and staring at his bedspread. The country became very angry at the queen for not coming to London, demanding that she left Balmoral to see the grieving crowds outside Buckingham Palace and Kensington Palace.

In 2022, on 9 September, Queen Elizabeth received the new prime minister, Liz Truss, at Balmoral and then passed away two days later. She was the first monarch to die in Scotland. Her final journey was made by car from Balmoral to Edinburgh, where she lay in state, before travelling on a plane to London. The last photo of the queen shows her in her green-and-white drawing room, wearing a tartan skirt, smiling and ready to welcome her fifteenth prime minister – working until the end.

Sandringham House

George V gave the first ever Christmas message, by radio: 'I am enabled, this Christmas Day, to speak to all my peoples throughout the Empire ... I speak now from my home and from my heart to you all.'

Sandringham House

'As there was all of England wherein to choose, I wish they had had a finer house in a more picturesque situation,' complained a lady-in-waiting on her first visit to Sandringham, with the newlyweds Edward ('Bertie'), the future King Edward VII and Alexandra, just after their honeymoon in 1863. The future Queen Alexandra, however, an 18-year-old bride, found the house very pleasant, writing to her sister that she considered it 'comfortable and cosy and not too large'. The couple spent the time walking about, discussing improvements to the garden. Sandringham Hall and its 7,700 acres of land had been newly purchased for Edward's marriage, with the sale secured just a few months before. Two years previously, Prince Albert had begun scouring the country for estates for his son, concerned about the 19-year-old's louche lifestyle, and convinced that marriage and a country estate would encourage him to settle down. Various estates were surveyed, including Houghton Hall, but a recommendation by the prime minister, Lord Palmerston, swayed Albert and Victoria to Sandringham. The death of the Prince Consort at the end of 1861 put a pause on matters, but as discussions heated up about a marriage to Princess Alexandra of Denmark, so did the efforts to buy a property, and Sandringham Hall was purchased at the end of 1862, for the rather large sum of £22,000. However, the house itself was somewhat run-down and too small to accommodate the hunting parties that Edward wished to host. Two years after he had moved in, in 1865, Edward instructed the architect A.J. Humbert to pull down the house and put up a new, more suitable building in its place, a red-brick house of three storeys. The only part of the former structure that remained was a conservatory. By the middle of 1875, the house was deemed too small once more and Humbert was brought in to extend it further.

The conservatory, which Edward had been using as a billiard room, was converted to a bowling alley. Edward was delighted with the renovations; he also extended the gardens, adding ornamental and kitchen gardens, and built staff cottages, a staff clubhouse, and kennels and stables. In 1886, Edward established the breeding stables and the Sandringham Stud, which was so important to Elizabeth II. He bought the brood mare

For the future king, Sandringham was a house where he could be away from the disapproving eyes of his mother. He hosted endless grand parties, at which there was much hunting, and mistresses were invited.

Perdita II in 1888 for £900, and two of her sons with the legendary racehorse St Simon were champion racers: Diamond Jubilee and Persimmon. The prince used his winnings on his horses to further extend Sandringham.

For the future king, Sandringham was a house where he could be away from the disapproving eyes of his mother. He hosted endless grand parties, at which there was much hunting, and mistresses were invited. Shooting became his focus: thousands of birds were killed a year and the game larder was the largest in Europe. Indeed, he even began the tradition of 'Sandringham Time', in which the clocks were set half an hour ahead, so that there was more light in the hunting season of the winter months. Edward spent more and more time at Sandringham in his later years. As a friend said: 'Up to the last year of his life he was continually improving his domain, repairing churches, spending money on the place in one way or another.' His eldest son, Albert Victor, died at Sandringham of pneumonia in 1892, less than a week after his twenty-eighth birthday, with his family and fiancée, Princess Mary of Teck, present at his bedside. Queen Alexandra kept the room in which he died as a shrine. Edward's second son, George, became his heir. When George married Mary of Teck, Edward gave them a house on the grounds as a wedding gift. Built to accommodate all of Sandringham's endless extra guests at parties, it had been known as 'Bachelor's Cottage' but was then named York Cottage, for George V, then Duke of York.

Not so much a cottage, but rather a large Victorian home – George declared it three Merrie England pubs joined together – it was rather cramped for the royal family and all their servants. Most of his children, including the future King George VI, were born at York Cottage. The youngest child, John, suffered from seizures and may have also had other learning disabilities; he was not invited to the coronation of his father and in 1916 was sent, at age 11, to live at Wood Farm, a small cottage overlooking the sea in a quiet part of the Sandringham Estate, where he lived with his own retainers, rarely seeing the family. They said it would upset his siblings too much to see him frequently. Queen Alexandra commented that he was proud of his house but lonely and longing for a companion, and his mother had local children brought in to play with him. John died after a severe seizure at Wood Farm in 1919.

When Edward VII died in 1910, he left a life interest in Sandringham to his wife, Queen Alexandra. The new king, George V, and his family crammed into York Cottage on the grounds, but he refused to ask his mother to move, saying that it was her house, as his father had built it for her. In 1925, Alexandra died, and King George and Queen Mary moved into Sandringham. The king loved Sandringham, as he was a keen shooter, and he enjoyed the peace away from London. He gave the first ever Christmas message, by radio, declaring: 'Through one of the marvels of modern science, I am enabled, this Christmas Day, to speak to all my peoples throughout the Empire.' As he said: 'I speak now from my home and from my heart to you all.' The king used to take the young Princess Elizabeth around the horses at the Sandringham Stud when she visited, and Christmas was usually celebrated at Sandringham, a tradition that Elizabeth II retained.

In January 1936, the king was very ill in his rooms at Sandringham and close to death. His doctors issued a bulletin: 'The king's life is moving peacefully towards its close.' However, he showed more strength than his physicians had expected and by 11 o'clock, it looked, his chief doctor thought, as if 'this last stage might endure for many hours'. *The Times* newspaper was waiting to publish the news of the king's death in the special morning edition. But the king was not yet dead. The chief doctor thought that there should be a 'brief final scene' in order to ensure the monarch's 'dignity and serenity', because having hours of life 'only exhausts the onloookers & keeps them so strained that they cannot avail themselves of the solace of thought, communion or prayer' – although he did not consult Queen Mary or the Prince of Wales on this, and it is highly unlikely that either would have agreed, particularly not the queen. So the doctor, Lord Dawson, 'decided to determine the end' and injected the king with a mix of morphia and cocaine, and he was pronounced dead at 11.55 p.m. – and the news was announced in *The Times*.

The new king Edward VIII spent little time at Sandringham, he preferred London and the company of Mrs Simpson. After he abdicated in December 1936, his brother George became king.

BBC

George VI was as fond of Sandringham as his father had been, since he found London and Buckingham Palace stressful. Christmas was often passed at Sandringham, as it had been when his father was alive. After war broke out in 1939, Sandringham was largely shut up, but the king did deliver his Christmas message from there; dressed in the uniform of the Admiral of the Fleet, he said: 'A new year is at hand. We cannot tell what it will bring. If it brings peace, how thankful we shall all be. If it brings us continued struggle we shall remain undaunted.' His final Christmas message, in 1951, was pre-recorded rather than live, due to his poor health. The king died in his rooms at Sandringham on 6 February 1952, and was discovered by his valet early in the morning. So, very rare for a monarch, it is unknown exactly when his reign ended and that of his daughter, Elizabeth II, began. The new queen was in Kenya and the Palace believed she had received the message that her father had died, so put the news out – however, she had not received it and did not know, and her secretary was told by a journalist. Prince Philip broke the news to her. The new queen flew back immediately to London.

The queen continued to celebrate Christmas at Sandringham, where the royal family would dine on a Sandringham turkey and make the traditional journey to St Mary Magdalene Church on the estate for Christmas Day service. It was all about joke presents for the royal family – Harry once gave the queen a bath cap. The queen would deliver her Christmas message from Sandringham, which, in 1957, was televised for the first time: 'I very much hope that this new medium will make my Christmas message more personal and direct,' she said as she read from the Long Library in Sandringham at 3 p.m. She would usually spend the winter period there, including commemorating the death of her father.

Sandringham was the site of an unfortunate incident with the queen's corgis in 2003. On arrival at Sandringham for Christmas, Princess Anne's bull terrier, Dotty, chased and attacked Pharos, one of Elizabeth's corgis. When Anne rang the bell, five corgis rushed down, Princess Anne's dogs dashed in and Dotty went for Pharos, one of the queen's older corgis. The decision was made to put Pharos down. Many of the queen's corgis were buried at Sandringham, in the pet graveyard begun by Queen Victoria for her collie, Noble. The queen's first-ever Corgi, Susan, a present on her eighteenth birthday, who even accompanied her on her honeymoon, is buried at Sandringham and her tomb bears the inscription: 'For almost Fifteen Years the faithful companion of the Queen.'

The Royal Pavilion

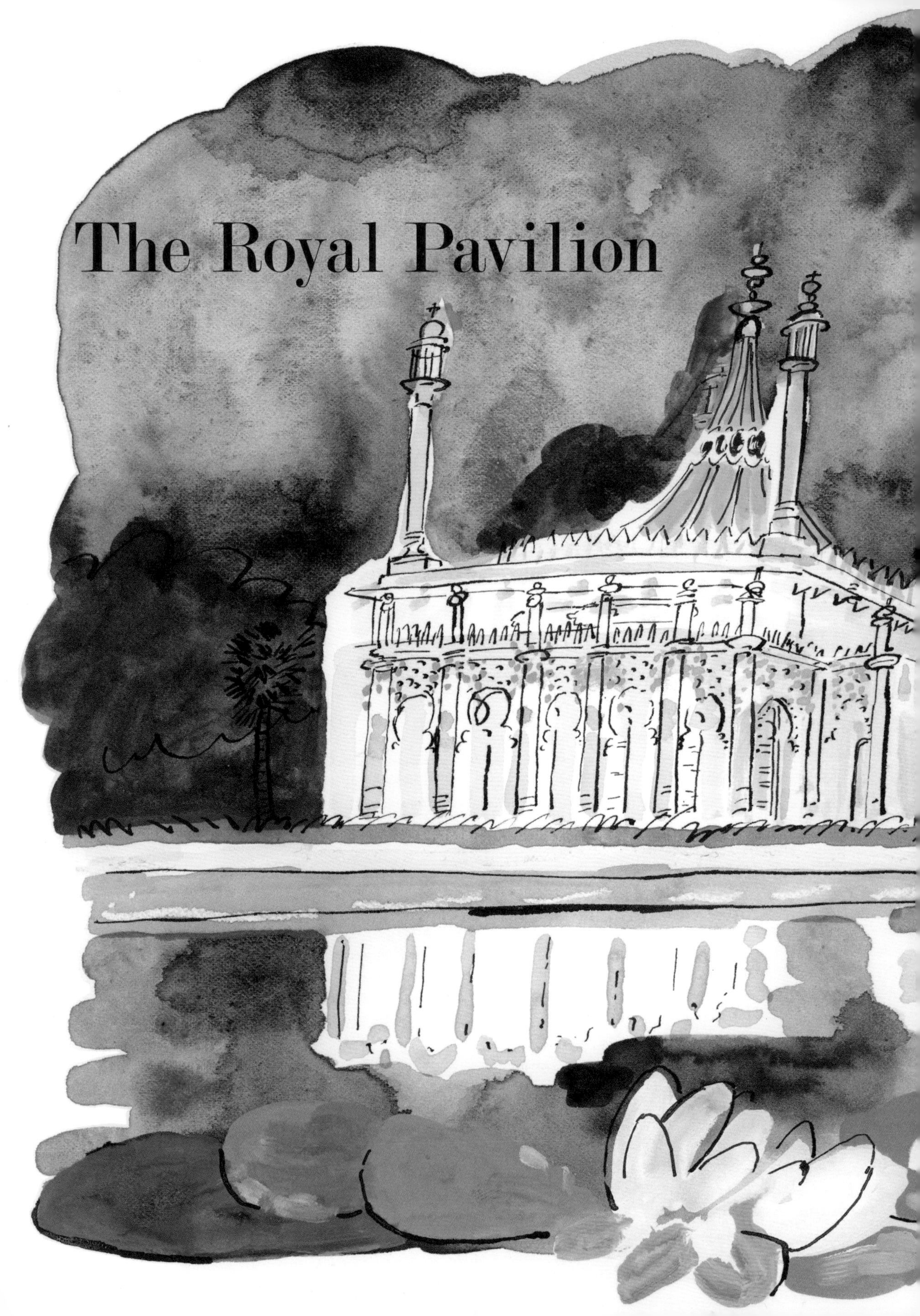

Commissioned by the Prince of Wales in the late-eighteenth and nineteenth centuries, the Royal Pavilion was the prince's dream house and an expression of his love of architecture and chinoiserie and the town of Brighton.

The Royal Pavilion

On 7 January 1817, the Prince Regent, the future George IV, threw a huge ball to celebrate the twenty-first birthday of his daughter, Charlotte. The Prince Regent was a legendary thrower of parties, hugely in debt due to his massive spending, and Brighton Pavilion was the scene of many of his most glamorous gatherings. There was just one problem with the grand ball: the guest of honour was not there. Princess Charlotte and her husband had chosen to spend her birthday quietly at their home, Claremont House, in Surrey. By April, the Princess was pregnant. As the only child of the Prince Regent, she carried the future of the royal family on her shoulders. George III had had seven sons and six daughters, and between them they had managed one legitimate child, Charlotte, and 56 illegitimate children. Only a few had bothered even to marry. The Prince Regent had married Princess Caroline only to get money from the king, and hated her on sight. The Duke of York had married but had no children, and he had been ridiculed in a court case over the selling of army commissions, in which his mistress Mary Anne Clarke, dressed in glamorous outfits, had recounted excerpts from his love letters. The Duke of Kent was happily ensconced with his mistress in Belgium, and had, no care for the succession.

For the Prince Regent, January was a time to party. Less than a fortnight after the ball for Princess Charlotte, he hosted a giant feast for the visit of the Grand Duke Nicolas of Russia, cooked by the great Antoine Carême, the first celebrity chef. It was served with all the courses on the table, in the style à la française. There were eight fish dishes, including the head of a great sturgeon in champagne, and 40 other main courses served around the fish; among them there was every possible bird or meat you could

imagine: from quail to beef, braised ducklings with lettuce, rabbit pie, supreme of venison, lamb with kidneys and chicken, as well as boar and a turkey. To finish, there were eight centrepieces, including the Royal Pavilion made out of pastry, a Welsh Hermitage made from sugar, a grand Parisian meringue, and towers of profiteroles – all surrounded by 32 desserts and other sides, including cherry jelly and whipped cream, apple and almond tartlets, and also scrambled egg and chicken. The Prince Regent knew how to throw a feast.

Commissioned by the Prince of Wales in the late-eighteenth and nineteenth centuries, the unique marvel of the Royal Pavilion was the prince's dream house and an expression of his love of architecture and chinoiserie and the town of Brighton.

When Prince George was first advised to make use of the salt water of Brighton's sea for his health, he found a community on the brink of gentrification. His patronage led to greater fame for the small town, and it was not long before society descended en masse on the seaside resort. Much of Brighton as we know it was built during his lifetime.

The Pavilion started off as a fairly standard converted farmhouse, although it was well located. In 1786 George rented it so he could indulge in various remedies for his gout, and also because it worked as a discreet location to meet his lover, Maria Fitzherbert. The two had been married the year before in an illegal ceremony – she was Catholic, and thus barred from marrying royalty.

It was not long before George felt that the building was not grand enough for someone of his status. The year after he managed to convince Parliament to cancel his debts and increase his income, he commissioned an expansion of the existing structure. Known as the Marine Pavilion, and built in a French-inspired style, the new building then grew further in the early years of the nineteenth century. Prince George also acquired much more land around his home, which he used for stables and a riding school.

To finish, there were eight centrepieces, including the Royal Pavilion made out of pastry, a Welsh Hermitage made from sugar, a grand Parisian meringue, and towers of profiteroles.

In 1811 George became the Prince Regent – his father, King George III, had become increasingly incoherent and was unable to perform his duties as monarch. The prince believed that he needed a more lavish and spacious home outside London, and so the Pavilion as we know it today was conceived. He hired famous architect John Nash to engage in a wholesale rebuilding of the entire estate – a massive undertaking, which began in 1815. Nash's project took almost a decade and converted the (previously rather traditional) building into a palace inspired by Islamic and Indian architecture. The interiors were also considered exotic at the time, as well as rather flashy – this was a building which was designed to demonstrate the range and variety of the Prince Regent's taste. No expense was spared in making it the most modern and convenient palace of the time, with particular focus being placed on the plumbing, heating and cooking facilities.

The interiors were considered exotic at the time, as well as rather flashy – this was a building which was designed to demonstrate the range and variety of the Prince Regent's taste.

Despite it being one of his favourite residences, and perhaps the creation for which he is best known now, George IV didn't manage to use his new Pavilion as much as he might have liked. He came to the throne in 1820, while the building was still under construction. Although the project was completed a couple of years later, there are only two official visits registered, in 1824 and 1827.

After George died in 1830, his son – crowned William IV – made more use of the royal residence in Brighton. He would often come with his wife, Queen Adelaide, although the extended retinue of the royal couple meant that the complex had to be expanded yet again. Most of the new buildings of this period no longer exist, but the designs and paperwork suggest that they were intended to accommodate the many servants and courtiers who were required to attend the royal couple.

Despite these extra buildings, Queen Victoria also felt that the Pavilion was too small for her purposes, especially as her family grew. It didn't help that the architectural style and interior decoration were beginning to be seen as old-fashioned. In 1850 she decided to sell the whole estate to the town of Brighton, and assumed the palace would be demolished. Almost everything that could be removed was packed up and sent to other royal palaces, and Brighton was left with an empty shell.

The Town Commissioners of Brighton refurbished the public-facing elements of the

George, the Prince Regent

Pavilion and opened it to the world, both as a place of historical and royal interest, and a venue for dances, weddings and functions. Before too long Queen Victoria realised that this public interest was good for the royal family, so she returned a number of original items – including furniture, paintings, chandeliers and more – to decorate the accessible areas of the building.

During the First World War, the British government took advantage of the Pavilion's Indian-inspired design and used it both as a hospital and a propaganda tool. Reconfigured, along with some neighbouring buildings, to house troops from the Indian army who had been fighting largely on the Western Front, much was made of the facilities provided.

Nowadays, the Pavilion is a Brighton landmark, open to the public and run by the city council. The domes and minarets and the beautiful interiors complete with original furniture and decorations take us back to the time of the Prince Regent and his spectacular parties in Brighton. The gardens, lovingly restored to their Regency grandeur, are a significant asset to Brighton, and the palace itself hosts art exhibitions, displays of historical items and occasional events. In the striking views of the domes and minarets, in the beautiful interiors complete with original furniture and fixings, we are provided with a direct connection with the fascinating Regency years.

Frogmore House

Queen Victoria gave Frogmore to her mother. When the latter died in 1861, the queen commissioned a grand Mausoleum by the lake and then one for her husband Albert. She herself was buried at Frogmore, with him.

Frogmore House

'I wonder you do not vote for putting us in a sack and drowning us in the Thames,' wrote Princess Sophia, daughter of George III, to her brother, the Prince of Wales. She and her sisters hated their life at Windsor, with its routine, and complained bitterly of life in a 'nunnery'. The queen was perfectly happy spending days at Frogmore House, reading, painting and embroidering, accompanied by her daughters; but they longed for freedom. Only one managed to marry during the life of the king. He simply could not bear to agree the marriages of his beloved daughters. And so, as their brothers partied and had too much freedom with mistresses, the princesses were tormented in their gilded prison.

Frogmore House in Home Park, Windsor, was initially so called because of all the frogs that lived nearby. The land of Frogmore was bought by Henry VIII, but the original house was built in the seventeenth century and occupied by various tenants, including George Fitzroy, 1st Duke of Northumberland, the illegitimate son of Charles II and Barbara Palmer. In 1792, George III bought it for Queen Charlotte as a Windsor retreat. Her daughters longed to escape, but the king had already stated: 'I cannot deny that I have never wished to see any of them marry: I am happy in their company, and do not in the least want a separation.' As soon as he began to fall ill with mental distress, the queen resolved not to mention the possible marriages, in case it would add to his anguish. She also had no wish to lose any of them to a foreign royal family – in the difficult days of the king's madness, she used them as a support. Princess Charlotte, daughter of the Prince of Wales, the only legitimate child produced by all of the children of George III at the time, called her aunts 'a parcel of old maids'. The king could be inappropriate and his behaviour verged on the abusive. Princess

Sophia wrote of her father: 'He is all affection and kindness to me, but sometimes an over kindness if you can understand that, which greatly alarms me.' As soon as their brother, George, became Prince Regent, the princesses were allowed to marry and two later did, but they did not have children.

Queen Victoria gave Frogmore to her mother. When the latter died in 1861, the queen commissioned a grand Mausoleum by the lake and then one for her husband Albert. She herself was buried at Frogmore, with him, rather than at St George's Chapel or Westminster Abbey. As Prince Harry declared in his memoir, Frogmore was 'the final resting place for so many of us', including Edward VIII and Wallis Simpson.

Frogmore House was occupied by various royals. In 1997, when the royal yacht was decommissioned, the Duke of Edinburgh created a *Britannia* room full of objects from the vessel.

In 1801, Queen Charlotte directed that a cottage be built near Frogmore House, known as Frogmore Cottage. It was generally occupied by staff or friends. Queen Victoria visited in 1875 and noticed 'an immense number of little frogs'. Her beloved servant, Abdul Karim, later lived there with his family. It was then divided into various dwellings for Windsor staff. In 2019, it was renovated into a single house for the newly married Prince Harry and Meghan Markle, the Duke and Duchess of Sussex. Even though all royals live in properties given to them by the Crown, renovated with Crown money – and millions are spent on them every year – the £2.4 million used to turn Frogmore into a single house (on work including wiring and a roof) caused mass outrage, and it was constantly used against the Sussexes. In 2020, the couple attempted to plan a model of royal work which would allow them to gain their own money; it was refused and they left Frogmore – although they paid the £2.4 million out of their own funds. At the funeral of Prince Philip, Prince Harry arranged to meet his brother and father in the Frogmore Gardens, by the 'old Gothic ruin', which, he said, was 'no more Gothic than the Millennium Wheel. Some clever architect, some bit of stagecraft'. The Sussexes would not return to their home as working royals.

Claremont House

George III's seven sons and six daughters had between them only produced this one legitimate child, Charlotte, and so she and her unborn baby bore the entire weight of the succession.

Claremont House

In November 1817, Princess Charlotte of Wales was awaiting the birth of her baby at Claremont House. She was young and healthy, only 21, and the country was delighted that she was expecting. Charlotte and her husband Leopold were a devoted couple; after a childhood made miserable by her warring parents – the Prince Regent, future George IV, and his estranged wife, Caroline – Charlotte valued Leopold's calm stability (even if he was fond of telling her what to do). The country had been thrilled when the news that Charlotte was pregnant had been put out, and spiralling bets were placed on the baby's sex. It was estimated that a boy would raise the stock market by 6 per cent, a girl by 2.5 per cent. George III's seven sons and six daughters had between them only produced this one legitimate child, Charlotte, and so she and her unborn baby bore the entire weight of the succession. Charlotte's father had tried to force her to marry the Prince of Orange, but she chose Prince Leopold, a totally impoverished but kind-hearted prince of Coburg, after meeting him at a party.

Charlotte's pregnancy proceeded well, and she and her husband lived quietly in their home, Claremont House in Surrey, bought for them as a wedding present by the nation and valued at a cost of £60,000. The house was a grand Palladian mansion built in 1774 by Capability Brown, on the site of a house built by architect and writer John Vanbrugh seventy years earlier. But by August 1817, Charlotte was deemed to have grown too large. There was concern the baby was getting too big and would be difficult to birth. Thus, the doctors decided that the best course of action was to put Charlotte on a strict diet to try to reduce the size of the baby. Of course, this could not work – all the strategy achieved was to weaken the princess in body and spirit. When she came to give birth, the politicians were called

to witness the event, as was customary. Sir Richard Croft, the doctor in charge, refused to let her eat. The physicians insisted that all was proceeding well because Charlotte had not made a sound. As the labour continued, she grew increasingly weaker, and her personal doctor suspected she would not be able to birth the child. He sent for an obstetrician, who might use forceps, but Croft refused to let him in. Charlotte was the future queen, giving birth to a future king. Had she simply been a consort, seen as expendable, the use of forceps would have probably occurred more quickly – forceps could save lives, but they were brutal and mothers died afterwards, usually from an infection due to the instruments not being fully clean. But with Charlotte, the doctors were as if frozen. The Prince Regent, who could have taken charge, was away shooting. She was alone, with only her terrified young husband to help her.

After a 56-hour labour, Charlotte finally gave birth at 9 o'clock at night to a large handsome boy – who was stillborn. Charlotte was heartbroken, but the doctor judged her to be physically fine. The politicians departed and Charlotte was encouraged to sleep. Leopold was sent to bed, exhausted, and probably took an opiate. Charlotte slept – but at midnight woke up with awful pains to the stomach and started vomiting. She was bleeding and finding it difficult to breathe. The doctor called for Leopold to be woken but he could not be stirred. Princess Charlotte clasped the hand of her husband's friend, Baron Stockmar. He rushed from the room to try again to rouse Leopold, but she called out for him. He returned and she was dead – she had died alone, as she had so often been in life.

The country was devastated. Shops hung black over their windows and closed for two weeks. Byron leaned out of his rooms on the Grand Canal in Venice and shouted so loudly that

Below Lord Byron

he was heard across the city. The country ran out of black material, and makers of fashionable goods begged the government to end the mourning period in case they went bankrupt. The Prince Regent was too much in shock to go to the funeral. His brothers, however, saw it as a starting gun. With no heir, it was up to them to relinquish their mistresses and find wives. The Duke of Kent set about ending his 27-year relationship with his Belgian mistress, who read in the newspaper that he was looking for a bride among the German princesses. Prince Leopold persuaded his widowed sister, Victoire, Princess of Leiningen, to accept the duke's proposal. Indebted, far from the throne as the fourth son, and 20 years her senior, he was hardly an engaging prospect, but they were married in May 1818 at Kew Palace, barely six months after Charlotte's death, in a joint wedding with the duke's elder brother and his German bride. As one wit put it about this sudden passion for marriage: 'Hot and hard each royal pair/Are at it going for the heir.' The Duchess of Kent's daughter was born at Kensington Palace the following year – Victoria, the future queen.

Leopold stayed in Claremont House, and frequently hosted his sister and niece Victoria, before he left to become king of the Belgians in 1831. Victoria used the house as an adult and gave it to the exiled king Louis Philippe and queen of France, after the king abdicated in 1848. He died at Claremont two years later.

Claremont House was first built by the playwright John Vanbrugh, who sold it to Thomas Pelham-Holles, Duke of Newcastle, who was prime minister twice. He later sold it to Robert Clive, rapacious governor of Bengal and key founder of the East India Company. He demolished it and rebuilt it, and after his death the house was sold to various owners, until it was bought for Charlotte and Leopold (at a too-high price) in 1816. In the early twentieth century, it was owned by Sir William Corry, director of the Cunard Line shipping company, and then became a school – as it still is today.

Tower of London

The Tower is a place of imprisonment and executions, and also where the monarch traditionally stayed before the coronation. But it is most famous as the home of the Crown Jewels.

Tower of London

On 12 February 1554, a young woman, barely 17 years of age, was taken to be executed on Tower Green, the private spot for execution. Lady Jane Grey, the nine-day queen and a pawn in the fight for dominance by her power-hungry family, had been put on trial the previous year for being put on the throne – instead of Mary I, Henry VIII's first child. Lady Jane's husband, Guildford Dudley, had been executed first outside the Tower, in the public execution space, and she had seen his remains brought back by cart as it passed under her window – much to her despair. She was taken to the block and begged the executioner: 'I pray you, dispatch me quickly.' She blindfolded herself but then could not find the block and cried out, 'What shall I do? Where is it?' She had to be helped to get into the right position. She was executed swiftly in one blow, a sacrifice to her family's ambition.

Nearly 20 years before, in 1536, Anne Boleyn had been executed in the same spot. She was arrested at Greenwich Palace and put on trial for adultery, and thus treason against the king, in the Tower of London. Even before the trial was completed, Henry sent for a swordsman from France to behead Anne – his only kindness, if it can be called that, sparing her the brutality of the executioner's axe. He laid out every demand for how he wished the execution to proceed, including the spot in the Tower where it was to take place (although it appears that his instructions were not obeyed).

When Anne entered the Tower after travelling from Greenwich, she was overcome with fear and begged the lords to believe that she was not guilty. They had no mercy; the die was cast by the king and she was handed to the constable. 'Do I go into a dungeon?' she asked, terrified. Anne was lodged in rooms in the Tower where she had stayed before her

grand coronation as queen, only three years previously, the moment of her triumph. The royal apartments had been renovated for her at the cost of over a million pounds. She had been six months pregnant and Henry was sure it was a boy – but Elizabeth was born and Anne's downfall began.

On Friday, 19 May, Anne was taken to the scaffold inside the Tower. George Boleyn and his fellow accused had already been executed at Tower Green, so she knew her fate. She refused to say she was guilty but praised the king: 'I am come hither to accuse no man, nor to speak anything of that, whereof I am accused and condemned to die, but I pray God save the king and send him long to reign over you, for a gentler nor a more merciful prince was there never: and to me he was ever a good, a gentle and sovereign lord.' It is likely she was complimentary about the king in an attempt to secure his favour for her infant daughter, Elizabeth, and her family. Anne was buried in an unmarked grave. The king was betrothed to Jane Seymour on the day after her execution and they were married at Whitehall 10 days later; it was as if Anne had never existed, and her daughter was immediately demoted to Lady Elizabeth rather than princess.

Henry had one further queen to send to the scaffold – Catherine Howard, his young fifth wife, who he also executed for adultery, and thus treason, in the Tower. When Anne of Cleves arrived in England for her wedding in January 1540, Henry was displeased by her and thought her not as fair as she had been represented. He had become infatuated with her pretty, young lady-in-waiting, Catherine Howard, who was probably around 17, although her exact age is not known and she could have been younger. Henry, as ever, seemed to treat his wife's ladies-in-waiting as sexual resources (there were few other women at court) and started showering presents on Catherine. The teenager had been found a place at court by her uncle, the Duke of Norfolk – also uncle to Anne Boleyn – although he had been so dismissive of Anne when Henry brought her down for adultery. Norfolk no doubt thought he could gain influence through another niece, and he was correct. By early July 1540, the marriage to Anne of Cleves had been annulled and she was deemed the king's sister. At the end of July, Henry married Catherine. He was 49; she was still a teenager. On the same day, he had Thomas Cromwell, architect of the Cleves marriage and the minister who had gathered the evidence against Anne Boleyn, executed at the Tower.

Henry was infatuated with Catherine, but less than 18 months after their wedding, she was sentenced to die at the Tower for adultery, and thus treason. Catherine defended herself with courage and explained that Francis Dereham, the man with whom she was accused of having had relations when she was very young, had raped her. But it was to no avail. Henry wanted her dead. She screamed hysterically when she was escorted to the barge that was to take her to the Tower, and spent the night before her execution practising how to lay her head upon the block. Her lady-in-waiting, Jane Rochford, who was the widow of George Boleyn (accused of adultery with his sister, Anne, and executed for it) had gone insane after lengthy interrogations about the queen's meetings with men. Her 'fits of frenzy' were so great that she couldn't be put on trial, but Henry was bent on executing her and so changed the law to allow those deemed insane to be executed. Jane was executed straight after Catherine Howard, on the same scaffold at Tower Green.

These executions were public. However, the most infamous deaths in the Tower are also its greatest mystery: the disappearance in 1483 of

the two princes, sons of Edward IV, who had been lodged in the White Tower. The king, Edward IV, had died in early April 1483 at the age of 41. His death had been unexpected and his son, Edward V, was crowned at the age of 12. The king's uncle, Richard Duke of Gloucester (later Richard III), put Edward into the Tower for his 'protection'. Of course, monarchs traditionally lodged at the Tower before coronation. Elizabeth, widow of Edward IV, fled to Westminster Abbey with her remaining children, for sanctuary, within a few weeks of her husband's death. Richard had her brother and her son by her first marriage arrested and put on trial for treason, so the queen was afraid. She hoped to keep her second son, Richard, with her, but the Duke of Gloucester had the nine-year-old transferred to the Tower. There was nothing she could do. The princes, young Edward and Richard, were apparently spotted playing outside the White Tower in the late spring of 1483, but by the summer, they were no longer sighted. Rumours spread across the country and Europe that they had been killed on the orders of Richard. In 1674, workmen digging up the stairs to the White Tower found a box containing the skeletons of two children. Although there was no identification, Charles II had the bodies buried in Westminster Abbey with a plaque, designed by Sir Christopher Wren, saying their 'long desired and much sought-after bones were found after a hundred and ninety years'.

The Tower is a place of imprisonment and executions, and also where the monarch traditionally stayed before the coronation. But it is most famous as the home of the Crown Jewels. These date back to the thirteenth century, and St Edward's Crown was named for Edward the Confessor, eleventh-century king. All, save one spoon, were melted down and sold by Oliver Cromwell after the Civil War. Once Charles II came to the throne, he ordered a whole new set of coronation regalia, including an orb, sceptre and another St Edward's Crown – but was fortunately given the spoon. All were used to great effect in his coronation in 1661. The jewels, made of gold and dripping in diamonds, were then taken to the Tower for storage and put on show to the public. But unlike now, when they are behind secure glass and visitors are moved quickly on a walkway, back then they were under rather lax seventeenth-century security – hence Thomas Blood's audacious effort to steal them.

For a fee, members of the public could visit the Tower and see the jewels, as the jewel-keeper took them out of the cupboard for handling. In spring 1671, a clergyman and his wife came to inspect them. When the wife suffered a fainting fit, the jewel-keeper, 77-year-old Talbot Edwards, who lived in the Tower with his wife and family, helped her to his lodgings upstairs and gave her a glass of water. They struck up a friendship and the clergyman suggested to Talbot that his nephew might be an excellent match for his unmarried daughter, so a meeting between the parents of the prospective couple was arranged for 9 May. But instead of a pleasant gathering over cakes, Talbot found himself tied up and beaten over the head with a mallet, as the 'clergyman' was in reality Thomas Blood, a former soldier for Cromwell who had dabbled in criminality since the Civil War (Blood's 'wife' had been a hired actress who faked her fainting episode). Blood, with his son and another gang member, stole the crown, orb and sceptre, and tried to make a getaway to the horses that another gang member was holding outside the Tower. To hide the items, Blood hammered down St Edward's Crown with a mallet, and his accomplice tried to stuff the orb down his trousers and cut the sceptre in half. But then the chance arrival of Talbot's son shook the gang; he managed to raise the alarm by shouting, 'Treason! The crown is stolen,' and gave chase, together with the Tower guards. The gang ran, firing their pistols, but were caught and arrested. 'It was a gallant deed, but it failed,' said Thomas Blood. Most strange of all was that Charles II, who had had the jewels made at huge expense only 10 years previously, pardoned Thomas Blood and granted him lands in Ireland worth a significant yearly income. Some might say it was an inside job.

The most famous parts of the Imperial State Crown include the Black Prince's Ruby on its front cross, which dates back to the fourteenth century and was demanded by the Black Prince, son of Edward III, as payment for helping King Pedro of Castile to quell a rebellion. Also renowned is the Stuart Sapphire – a huge sapphire with which James II ran off when he was deposed (it was later bought back) – and St Edwards's Sapphire, said to have been taken from Edward the Confessor's ring in 1163. Last but not least, the giant Cullinan diamond, found in 1905, is the biggest diamond ever discovered; it was divided into nine large pieces (and over 90 small diamonds), and one giant section is in the sovereign's sceptre and another at the front of the Imperial State Crown.

The Imperial State Crown is worn by the sovereign and new versions of it are made for most coronations, with the current version very like that made for Queen Victoria in 1838. Charles II's version survived the efforts of Thomas Blood and his gang to steal it and there have been various mishaps – including being dropped on the floor at Queen Victoria's coronation by the Duke of Argyll. The young queen decided it looked 'all crushed and squashed like a pudding that had sat down'. The St Edward's Crown is the crown used at the moment of coronation and it is exceedingly heavy, at 5lb (just over 2kg), so much so that after Charles II commissioned a new one

in 1661, it was used for just under 30 years and then not used again until the twentieth century for the coronations of George V, George VI, Elizabeth II and Charles III. The late Queen Elizabeth declared it could 'snap your neck' – monarchs are much relieved to be able to take it off after the moment of coronation and put on the Imperial State Crown, which is half its weight. The St Edward's Crown is always used to crown the sovereign alone – with the exception of Anne Boleyn. When she was crowned in 1533, heavily pregnant, she was given St Edward's Crown, no doubt to legitimise her, as she faced so much opposition, and also to crown the son that Henry VIII was sure she bore. But her child was a girl, Elizabeth, and Anne would be executed not three years after her coronation. The St Edward's Crown was not used by Mary II – William, her husband, got to wear it, carry the traditional orb and sit in the Coronation Chair. Even though Mary's was the claim, as James II's daughter, she was treated in terms of regalia as consort.

In 2014, after visiting the display of poppies in the Tower moat, one for each Commonwealth soldier who had died in the First World War, Harry, William and Kate were offered a tour of the Tower. It seems surprising that it was then that Harry saw the Crown Jewels for the first time in his life; he stared at St Edward's Crown and was struck by how 'magical' it seems, with a strange internal glow. As he concluded: 'You couldn't help but feel that a ghost, encountered late at night in the Tower, might have a similar glow.'

One of 36 castles he constructed across the country, the Tower of London was built by William the Conqueror as a huge fortress to secure his position after invading in 1066, and to cow and instil fear in his new people. The White Tower was built in the late eleventh century, with grand apartments for the king. It took about 20 years to build the Tower, which was expanded by successive monarchs, and although it was a royal palace, it was generally unpopular with the people. In the reign of King Richard II, those involved in the Peasants' Revolt besieged the castle with the king inside it and when the young King Richard rode out to meet Wat Tyler, some of his supporters broke into the castle and stole from the Jewel House.

By Tudor times, the Tower was more prison than royal residence. But so many royals were sent there that perhaps there was some overlap. Princess Elizabeth was herself imprisoned in the Tower by her half-sister, Mary I. Elizabeth had dodged being accused of treason while her brother was king, as she defended herself staunchly over Thomas Seymour's attempt to marry her after the death of his wife (he had groomed and assaulted Elizabeth while living with her as Katherine Parr's husband, so she was guiltless, but Tudor society was not forgiving) and accusations of having known

of his plots. Elizabeth, only 15, said she knew nothing and escaped being taken to the Tower. But under the reign of Mary I, Henry VIII's daughter with Catherine of Aragon, Elizabeth was under suspicion and in real trouble. Less than a year after Mary rode into London in triumph in August 1553, with Elizabeth at her side, deposing Lady Jane Grey, a rebellion led by Thomas Wyatt broke out, aiming to kill Mary and put Elizabeth on the throne. The rebels were was routed, the conspirators were arrested and Elizabeth was sent to the Tower. There she was interrogated about how much she had known about the plot. It was painfully obvious to Mary that her sister was a constant threat to the stability of her reign – and her effort to institute a Catholic sovereignty. Lady Jane Grey's father was accused of being involved in the rebellion and thus Lady Jane Grey, whom Mary had imprisoned but did not want to execute, was doomed. Just over a week after Wyatt was arrested, Lady Jane Grey was executed at the Tower. In the following month, Elizabeth was taken to the Tower by boat from Whitehall, after attempting to stave off the journey by writing a long letter to her sister, known as the 'Tide Letter'. She was terrified: she walked past the scaffold where Lady Jane Grey had been executed and was lodged in the royal apartments, where her mother had stayed before she was beheaded. Elizabeth defended herself bravely and there was no real evidence that she had been involved. Also, executing a royal – and her own sister at that – would have been shocking and could have instigated more rebellion; Mary decided to show mercy and keep Elizabeth under house arrest in Woodstock for the next year. Elizabeth wisely lay low for the rest of her sister's reign.

Elizabeth later stayed in her mother's apartments in the Tower before her own great coronation, in which she paraded through the streets of London in triumph. When she came to the throne, Elizabeth I did use the Tower to execute her enemies. Her final execution was the Earl of Essex, once her devoted admirer, who was tried for treason after attempting to lead a rebellion against her. He pleaded not to be killed in public and was permitted to die on Tower Green. The executioner held up the earl's head and called: 'God Save the Queen'.

In the early morning of 5 November 1605, James I ordered a search of Parliament after being tipped off about a conspiracy against him. Guy Fawkes was found underneath the building with gunpowder. He declared his name was John Johnson and refused to talk. He was taken to the Tower and the king instructed he be subjected to light torture at first and then, if he continued to say nothing, to be put on the rack. By 7 November, Fawkes admitted his part in the Gunpowder Plot to kill the king and gave his real name – and was forced to make a confession, which he signed.

After the Tudor period, the Tower was much less used as either a royal residence or a prison. The last king to stay in the Tower on the night before his coronation was Charles II. From the mid-eighteenth century, no one else was executed there – until Carl Lody, who was accused of being a German spy and executed by firing squad in the early years of the First World War.

The Tower is famous for its ravens and its Yeoman Warders or 'Beefeaters'. The latter were initially part of the monarch's personal guard, or the Yeoman of the Guard, and Henry VIII declared that some would remain to guard the Tower. Henry's personal guards were called 'Beefeaters' because they were allowed to consume as much beef as they desired from the king's table. Every day, the Yeoman Warders lock and unlock the Tower in the Ceremony of the Keys.

In 1279, Edward II moved the Mint to the Tower and most coins were made there until 1810. Its security deterred forgers and robbers; the workers at the Mint were kept strictly separated from the guards and other inhabitants of the Tower, and they were watched. Until 1600, coins were made by hand and using toxic chemicals: it was tough and dangerous work at high temperatures. A worker would place a coin between two engraved stamps and another worker would bash it with a hammer – they had to be alert! In the reign of Henry VIII, a potter fell asleep over his pots and could not be woken for 14 days, probably knocked out by poisonous gas. The Mint was vital: when the Parliamentarians seized the Tower early in the Civil War, they had the Mint, and thus a key advantage. In Charles II's reign new machinery was installed in the Tower of London to create machine-struck coins, which were thicker, more uniform and harder to forge – not only due to uniformity, but also to milling and edge lettering. It was still hard work; the machines (powered by horses) struck about 30 finished coins per minute and the workers had to flick them away with their middle finger, while using the thumb and index finger to add a fresh blank – injuries were common. In the early nineteenth century, the Royal Mint moved to Tower Hill and then to its current home in Wales in the 1960s.

In 1235, three leopards (they may have been lions) arrived as a gift for Henry III so the king decided to start a menagerie in the Tower. A polar bear arrived 15 years later from the king of Norway. It was allowed to hunt and swim for fish in the Thames, although it was always chained. The king of France sent an elephant in 1255, but it died within a few years – perhaps being fed red wine did not help. The animals were specially housed by Edward I in a tower called the Lion Tower and the collection grew, particularly that of lions, which survived the bad English weather and food. Henry VIII was given an old brown bear, Max, by the Emperor Maximilian and yet more lions. By the early seventeenth century, there were pumas, a tiger and a jackal, and James I expanded the lions' area so that more visitors could see them in their yard. The public were allowed to enter in the eighteenth century; the price was three pence (later nine pence), or a cat or dog to be fed to the lions. In 1826, 150 animals were given to found the new London Zoo in Regent's Park, and other animals were sold before the menagerie was finally closed in 1835. Now, the Tower contains wire sculptures by Kendra Haste commemorating the animals kept there.

Now overseen by Historic Royal Palaces the tower commemorates all those who lived and died there. Elizabeth I is a perfect example: imprisoned as princess, triumphant as queen.

Clarence House

SALMON
SALMON
SALMON

The house will have the rare distinction of having been home to at least three generations of monarchs – Queen Elizabeth II, King Charles III and William.

Clarence House

The wedding of Princess Elizabeth and Prince Philip in November 1947 was, according to Winston Churchill, a 'splash of colour on the hard road on which we have to travel'. The couple's wedding breakfast was produced using ration foods, like pigeon, and the ingredients for the cakes were donated by the Girl Guides of Australia. The young couple moved into Clarence House – along with their wedding gifts, over 25,000 of them. Among the presents were a cinema, 500 tins of pineapple, a Sèvres porcelain dinner set from the government and people of France, 10 carpets, a box of Kentish apples, a set of drinking chocolate cups from the Pope, a wooden writing desk from the government of New Zealand, and a glass bowl from President Truman and the First Lady. The princess also received a gold and jade necklace from the king of Egypt, an enamel box with a singing bird from the queen of Romania, tins of salmon, 24 pairs of gloves and a silver basket from all girls living in Twickenham who were named Elizabeth, Alexandra or Mary.

Prince Philip took charge of the renovations after they moved in. Prince Charles was born at Buckingham Palace, but Princess Anne was born at Clarence House and the young couple were very happy – and hoped to spend many years there. However, less than six years after their marriage, George VI died and Elizabeth became queen, so they had to move to Buckingham Palace.

Built between 1835 and 1837, Clarence House was designed by master architect John Nash and has been the home of numerous prominent royals. Situated close to both Buckingham Palace and St James's Palace, its convenience and relative privacy mean that the royals enjoy living there. The house was commissioned by William Henry, Duke of Clarence, for whom it is named, who was to become King William IV. After his ascension to the throne, William remained unconvinced by the ageing and restrictive apartments at St James's Palace, so decided to stay at his modern townhouse. As he still needed to entertain at the main royal palace, he asked for a new passage to be built between Clarence House and the state apartments, so that he could more easily transfer between his home and his place of work. The passage still exists today, enabling the royals to move between palaces.

Clarence House was designed by master architect John Nash. Situated close to both Buckingham Palace and St James's Palace, its convenience and relative privacy mean that the royals enjoy living there.

The house was originally connected to the residence of William's sister, Princess Augusta, who inherited the whole complex after his death. This part of the structure was demolished after her passing, meaning that Clarence House opened up on the gardens of St James's. Queen Victoria's mother then moved in and made further changes to the building, allowing her to enter and exit directly to the Mall, rather than through the more public Stable Yard Road. Queen Victoria and her children would often visit the newly redecorated house from their residence, Buckingham Palace.

It was one of Victoria's children who next lived in the house, moving in five years after the death of his grandmother in 1861. Alfred, Duke of Edinburgh, and his Russian wife, Marie, lived at Clarence House for over 30 years, and oversaw yet more alterations to the design, decoration and structure of the building. It now appeared to be part of St James's Palace, at least from the outside – but the interior remained distinct, and a place where the inhabitants could feel as if they were separated from the hustle and bustle of the main working palace.

Another son of Victoria – Arthur, Duke of Connaught (also, later, Duke of Edinburgh) – was the next inhabitant, until his death in 1942. For a short period during his time there, the house also served as a repository for the library of the School of Oriental and African Studies, although the onset of the Second World War meant that the books were evacuated from London. Luckily so, for Clarence House was damaged during the Blitz, presumably due to its proximity to both Buckingham Palace and St James's. Arthur died of natural causes during the war, and the building was handed over to be the headquarters of the Red Cross and the

On your 100th Birthday
all the family join with
me in sending you our
loving best wishes
for this special day.
Lilibet

St John Ambulance Brigade. The former used it as an administration base to contact prisoners of war overseas and staged an exhibition on their stories.

After the death of her father, King George VI, the new queen and her immediate family decamped to Buckingham Palace, which had replaced St James's as the primary residence of the monarch, transferring Clarence House to her mother and sister. Princess Margaret thus lived there in the hard years after her father's death, and it was there that she made her decision not to marry Peter Townsend. Instead, she would marry Lord Snowdon in 1960 and move into an apartment in Kensington Palace. Queen Elizabeth, the Queen Mother, continued to live there until her death in 2002. She received a telegram from her daughter on the occasion of her hundredth birthday, hand-delivered to the front gate of Clarence House, having been sent from Buckingham Palace, just down the road.

She received a telegram from her daughter on the occasion of her hundredth birthday, hand-delivered to the front gate of Clarence House, having been sent from Buckingham Palace, just down the road.

Following his grandmother's death, then Prince Charles, moved into Clarence House in 2003. His sons William and Harry also officially resided there for much of the next decade, meaning that the house will have the rare distinction of having been home to at least three generations of monarchs – Queen Elizabeth II, King Charles III and William. William and Kate's engagement interview was conducted in Clarence House, and the bride-to-be wore a blue dress to match her sapphire and diamond engagement ring, once Princess Diana's. William said he had been carrying it around Kenya with him until he popped the question; indeed, he had been 'planning it for a while but as every guy out there will know, it takes a certain amount of motivation to get yourself going'.

Although Buckingham Palace remains the official home of the monarchy, it currently requires significant restoration. Although Buckingham Palace is the official home of the monarchy, it required restoration, and so King Charles continued to live at Clarence House in the years following his accession.

Glamis Castle

In Macbeth, *Macbeth himself lives at the castle as Thane of Glamis, but the real King Macbeth probably did not.*

Glamis Castle

Cecilia Bowes-Lyon, the mother of the future Queen Elizabeth, the Queen Mother, was unconvinced by royalty. She suggested that people had to be 'fed the royals, like sea lions fed fish'. But despite comparing the royals to fish, her home Glamis Castle saw many important royal moments.

Glamis Castle was at first a hunting lodge. In *Macbeth*, Macbeth himself lives at the castle as Thane of Glamis, but the real King Macbeth probably did not. King Malcolm II of Scotland died at Glamis, possibly murdered. He'd had a bloody rise to the throne, gaining it in 1005 after defeating and killing his cousin King Kenneth III in battle. After he died in 1034, his grandson took the throne as Duncan I, but five years later he was killed in battle by Macbeth, who then married a daughter of Kenneth III, gaining a claim to the throne (he may have already been related through his mother to Kenneth). He was later defeated and killed in battle by Duncan's son, Malcolm III. Shakespeare wrote *Macbeth* for James I (James VI of Scotland), and it is possible that he heard the story from Patrick, 9th Lord Glamis, who accompanied James I to England – and perhaps told stories putting his own castle centre stage, since the play differs greatly from the written source of *Holinshed's Chronicles*. Patrick was well connected to the king; his wife, Anne Murray, had probably been a mistress to the monarch, and was in fact described as such to William Cecil, chief minister to Elizabeth I. King James and his queen had been due to attend Patrick and Anne's wedding at Stirling Castle in 1595, but the queen fell ill and they missed it. Perhaps just as well. James had written poetry, 'A Dream on his Mistress my Lady Glamis' and a 'Complaint', bemoaning her absence from court, which he described as so terrible that it turned the court into a hell, a Hades, without her; he declared: 'The Court is a garland missing its chiefest flower.' Perhaps not the queen's

King Macbeth

preferred reading. The king gave Anne trunks of expensive clothes, including a silver cloth dress.

Patrick set about rebuilding and renovating the castle in the early seventeenth century. In the early eighteenth century, it was inherited by John Lyon, Earl of Strathmore and Kinghorn, who used the fortune of his wife, Mary Eleanor Bowes, a coal heiress, to rebuild much of the castle. In 1900, Lady Elizabeth Bowes-Lyon was born the ninth child and youngest daughter of Claude Bowes-Lyon, Earl of Strathmore and Kinghorn. During the First World War, Glamis became a field hospital for wounded soldiers and Elizabeth helped with nursing them. After the war ended, there was such a shortage of men that most young women took any proposal they could get. But when Bertie, Duke of York and the second son of the king, proposed to Elizabeth in 1921, she refused him. She had at least one other suitor, and she was also unsure about marrying into the royal family. As she put it, she was concerned she would never again be 'free to think, act or speak as I feel I really ought to'. Queen Mary visited Glamis, but even she could not change anyone's mind. Bertie asked Elizabeth again in early 1922, after she had been bridesmaid to his sister. She refused once more. Undeterred, he asked a third time in 1923, and she finally accepted. At Westminster Abbey, she laid her bouquet on the tomb of the Unknown Warrior, in memory of her brother, who had been killed in the First World War. Royal brides since have done the same – but on leaving, rather than entering, the Abbey.

Elizabeth II was born in 1926 and Margaret in 1930 at Glamis Castle. The tiny Princess Elizabeth was delighted by her new sister and tried to wheel her about in her pram to show her off. The family lived a quiet royal life in their Piccadilly townhouse – until Edward VIII abdicated. Bertie then became King George VI and Elizabeth became queen – truly one of the 'fish' about which her mother had been so dubious.

Conwy Castle

To approach Conwy by road, rail or sea is to understand just how dominant and unmissable this medieval castle must have been.

Conwy Castle

Located right on the edge of the North Wales coast, Conwy Castle is a truly impressive presence in the medieval town which is named after it. Commissioned around 1283 by King Edward I as part of his plans for the conquest and subjugation of the Welsh people, it was designed by James of St George, born in Savoy but responsible for some of the great Welsh castles, including Harlech and Beaumaris. The work was completed by 1287, and the cost of the castle, including the simultaneous building of a great wall around the town, came to £15,000 – a great sum for the royal coffers at the time.

Built on the site of Aberconwy Abbey, a hugely important place of worship for North Wales, the castle was intended to be a striking example of English power in the region. The Abbey was moved further up the Conwy valley to a new site funded by Edward – who knew that even though he wanted to show his power, he also had to show his piety.

In 1295 a Welsh rebellion sealed Edward up inside the castle for the winter months, with the only source of provisions a dangerous approach from the sea. Some claim the king asked that his store of wine be given to the defenders, but this is probably unlikely. It appears as if the siege and subsequent brief visits by Edward II and Richard II were the only times when royalty resided in Conwy Castle, although many other senior members of the court also stayed. Thus, the surviving residential rooms are the most complete to have been inhabited by medieval monarchy anywhere in England and Wales.

Despite these royal visits, Conwy Castle fell into periods of decline and occasional repair, notably under the orders of the Black Prince in the mid-fourteenth century. Nevertheless, it remained an important stronghold, and was again captured by the Welsh as part of Owain Glyndŵr's rebellion. It was also used variously as a prison, a storehouse and a garrison, and

Edward I

was important enough to Henry VIII for him to invest more money and time in repairs to the structure. Its last use as a working castle was during the English Civil War, when it was once again repaired and reinforced by Royalists, before a defection led to it being controlled by supporters of Parliament.

Another siege led to eventual victory by the Royalists, and yet more hasty repairs, but in the aftermath of Charles II's restoration it was decided to put the castle beyond military use, and key parts of the structure were systematically demolished. Not long afterwards the owner, the Earl of Conway, stripped all valuables from the building, which fell into severe disrepair.

The attraction of the ruins, however, became more and more evident over the following centuries. Still a massive and imposing presence on the North Wales coast, the remnants of the castle became a favourite subject for artists, including J.M.W. Turner. As its fame grew and tourism became more fashionable, aided by the expansion of the rail network, the town of Conwy realised the value of what it had. The site was made more accessible, and various repairs and reconstructions were carried out throughout the nineteenth century, and the castle was handed over officially to the town of Conwy in 1865. A further large round of repairs and research was carried out after the Second World War, leaving us with the castle as we know it today. To approach Conwy by road, rail or sea is to understand just how dominant and unmissable this medieval castle must have been. You can make a complete circuit of its battlements, unlike many other remaining medieval castles, and explore the royal residences and servants' quarters. Looking out over the walls of Conwy, to the sea and the mountains, is perhaps as close as we can get to understanding how these magnificent structures impacted the people who lived in and nearby them.

Edinburgh Castle

The castle was occupied by one side or the other during various conflicts: normally – but not always – between supporters of the English throne and opponents of whoever was currently sitting on it.

Edinburgh Castle

Standing high above the capital of Scotland, Edinburgh Castle is one of the most imposing and striking of the royal palaces. Built atop Castle Rock, which has been on-and-off the site for some sort of fortification since at least the Iron Age, the strategic and military value of the site is clear. It should be no surprise, then, that it would be home to a succession of rulers and royals over the centuries, and that such a vibrant and important city would grow up around it.

However, the location and the obvious importance of the site also mean that Edinburgh Castle is said to have been frequently besieged over the years – more than any other place in Britain – and has been built, damaged, expanded, rebuilt and reimagined many times. The current building is a tapestry of architectural and building styles, giving it a style all of its own.

The first monarch we can be sure made the castle their base of power was King David I, in the early twelfth century, although there are conflicting reports that his father, King Malcolm III, also resided there. However, it is clear that David used the site as a starting point for his wide reforms of the political and power structure of Scotland. His grandson, Malcom IV, also spent much time at the castle, cementing its position as the keystone of Scottish royal power.

Such an important and prominent building has naturally been used as a playing piece in the many centuries of conflict between Scotland and England. For a brief period in the late twelfth century, it was ceded to the English as part of a surrender treaty, before being returned as a dowry present, and in the last years of the thirteenth century it was taken over wholesale by the English King Edward I. Over the following centuries the castle changed hands on numerous occasions, and witnessed some of the most important moments of Scottish history.

These included the first fireworks display in Scotland, in 1507; the Black Dinner, at which two young sons of the powerful Douglas family were executed in the presence of the 10-year-old King James II, in order to temper the power of his rivals; the delivery of massive cannon Mons Meg, still one of the biggest in the world, in 1454, now on display in the castle; the escape of Alexander Stewart, Duke of Albany, via a well-placed window and a rope, and his subsequent return at the head of a besieging army in 1482; the birth to Mary, Queen of Scots of her son James, who would later unite Scotland and England; and the subsequent 'Lang Siege' of 1571–73, in which supporters of Mary occupied the castle and used its position to bombard Edinburgh before seeing their fortifications – and a large part of the castle – destroyed around them by English cannon fire.

Despite this extensive damage, the castle was redesigned and repaired, but over the next two centuries this pattern was repeated again and again. The castle was occupied by one side or the other during various conflicts: normally – but not always – between supporters of the English throne and opponents of whoever was currently sitting on it. On other occasions the two sides were fighting over religion. Whatever the conflict, the cycle of destruction and refortification went on, until the castle was a mishmash of remnants of previous structures and new buildings. Due to the importance of the site – and its obvious role as a magnet for aggression – each new iteration tended to be more military and defensive than the last.

This cycle ended with the second Jacobite rebellion in 1745: the last time – so far – the castle was put under siege. After Bonnie Prince Charlie failed to take the castle, it remained in the hands of the existing garrison. But in the following years it continued to be heavily fortified, in part due to the memory of previous conflicts. No one wanted to be the person who saw the castle taken again. It was also used to garrison soldiers, hold prisoners of war, store munitions and act as a locus for Scottish power. But without the need to rebuild following assault and destruction, the structure of the various buildings began to decline. After a mass escape of prisoners of war in 1811, it was decided that the castle was no longer fit for purpose, and it began to be seen as a tourist attraction and place of historical interest.

In 1818, the famous novelist Sir Walter Scott was given permission to search the castle for the lost crown of Scotland. It was found, along with the rest of the 'Honours of Scotland', in a forgotten locked chest, and they were put on display shortly afterwards. This was perhaps the moment which cemented the view of the castle as a place of history, rather than somewhere still in use.

There were exceptions, though; a garrison of soldiers remained in place until 1923, and both the First and Second World Wars saw the ancient prison cells in use again, notably for downed German fighter pilots. Even today, the army still maintain a presence in the castle and manage the military museums. But there can be no doubt that it was during the mid-nineteenth century that the castle's purpose changed from defensive to attractive, as it was opened up to tourists and those with an interest in history.

The late nineteenth and early twentieth centuries saw the focus move to rebuilding and restoring the castle's heritage, leaving us with the estate as we see it now. A mixture of historic buildings, some restored and some not, alongside its place as Scotland's busiest tourist attraction, mean that Edinburgh Castle is one of the most interesting and vibrant of Britain's royal palaces. To watch the Royal Edinburgh Military Tattoo in August, or to hear the almost-daily firing of the One o'Clock Gun to give ships in the harbour an accurate timing, is to be a part of history.

Falkland Palace

Generations of Stuart royals spent much time at Falkland. It was often a site for extensive revelry, and James IV, in particular, was partial to exotic entertainments.

Falkland Palace

Located in Fife, Falkland Palace is one of the most historic of the Scottish royal palaces. Originally the site of a hunting lodge in the twelfth century, due to its defensible location and rich surroundings, it later became a proper castle. The chaotic conflicts between the Scottish clans, which lasted for many years, meant that a castle which could be easily defended and support itself in times of war was a vital asset, and the Clan MacDuff held the estate for much of this period. It was then passed on to one of the most prominent members of the Stuart family: Robert, Earl of Menteith.

The Stuarts were closely linked with the royal family at the time, but Robert – son of King Robert II – made the mistake of imprisoning his nephew David, son of Robert III, at Falkland in the late fourteenth century. David would die at the castle, and although Robert managed to convince the Parliament of Scotland that he was not responsible for David's death, the scandal deeply damaged his branch of the family. In the end Falkland passed to the royal Stuarts, with King James I claiming it as his own in 1424.

The subsequent generations of Stuart royals spent much time at Falkland, and so it was a frequent recipient of their money and renovation efforts. They enjoyed its relative seclusion and rich hunting grounds, and by the early sixteenth century the building had become a truly lavish palace, largely built in the Renaissance style. It was often a site for extensive revelry, and James IV, in particular, was partial to exotic entertainments. These included the presentation of a live seal, the release of wild boar into the grounds, and a succession of musical and dramatic presentations.

Later Scottish monarchs continued the extravagant and pleasing expansions of the complex, with James V ordering the construction of what is now the oldest

A tennis player from the Stuart court

surviving royal tennis court in the country – an amenity which was apparently much used by his daughter Mary, Queen of Scots, who was a relatively frequent visitor in the early years of her reign. After Mary's imprisonment by Elizabeth I, her son James VI (later James I of England and Ireland) spent some time at Falkland, including using it as a secure and isolated refuge from the Black Death.

James VI later handed over Falkland as part of his dowry for his marriage to Princess Anne of Denmark, but it remained a key part of the royal estates in Scotland. Many monarchs and powerful figures enjoyed the hospitality of Falkland in later years, until Cromwell's forces occupied it during the Civil War and a major fire damaged it beyond habitation. Although many elements of the original buildings remained *in situ* – including walls, some ceilings, the tennis court, much of the chapel and gardens – they were considered unusable.

Thus, the ruins were largely ignored until the late nineteenth century, when the Marquis of Bute acquired the estate and began a lengthy process of repair and restoration. His successors continued his work, with various archaeology and research projects adding to the accuracy of the newest version of the palace.

The current buildings will never be able to recapture the glory of the Renaissance palace and grounds, but remain a remarkable demonstration of the ability of the royal palaces to attract and inspire visitors. Parts of the palace's structure were used in the TV series *Outlander*, the tennis court is one of the most historically important examples of its kind, and the gardens are now designed to focus on sustainable practices; the palace itself is managed by the National Trust for Scotland. It may not be as imposing as some of the other royal homes, but Falkland Palace is an important part of Scottish royal history, as well as a beautiful estate.

Hatfield House

In 1536, the future Elizabeth I was at home in Hatfield House. But the fall of Anne Boleyn changed everything. Elizabeth, two years and eight months old, was told that she was no longer Princess Elizabeth, but Lady Elizabeth.

Hatfield House

In 1536, Princess Elizabeth, the future Elizabeth I, was at home in Hatfield House. Her father, Henry VIII, had forced her half-sister, Mary, to wait on her. But the fall of Anne Boleyn changed everything. Anne was executed at the Tower and Elizabeth, just two years and eight months old, was swiftly told that she was no longer Princess Elizabeth, but Lady Elizabeth. Mary was released from serving her younger sister – they were both disgraced.

Hatfield House was built in 1497 by the Archbishop of Canterbury, but was later seized as a church property by Henry VIII and used as a palace for his children. Elizabeth spent much of her childhood at Hatfield and felt at home there. After her father died, she was sent to live with her stepmother, Katherine Parr, in her house in Chelsea. There she was sexually harassed by Katherine Parr's new husband, Thomas Seymour, who hoped to gain control over Elizabeth. Katherine died in childbirth in September 1548 so Elizabeth, just 15, and her household moved back to Hatfield. However, now that his wife had conveniently died, Seymour was determined to marry Elizabeth; he was obsessed with power. Early the following year, on the night of 16 January, he tried to break into the rooms of Edward VI in Hampton Court Palace, via Edward's garden. One of Edward's dogs barked, and Seymour shot and killed it. Seymour, arrested with a pistol near the king's apartments, couldn't look more guilty and he was sent to the Tower. Seymour's brother, the Lord Protector, was convinced there was a plot against the king and everyone around Seymour was under suspicion – including Elizabeth. When her governess was arrested, Elizabeth realised she was in grave danger. Sir Robert Tyrwhitt was sent to Hatfield to place Elizabeth under house arrest and interview her. He said that he saw in her face that she was guilty, but he could not get her to admit

Below Lady Elizabeth

anything. She stood fast and admitted nothing. She knew she risked death – execution, like Seymour. She outwitted them. But she had been terribly burned by Seymour and how close she had come to catastrophe. Her father had executed her mother and her stepmother, and Elizabeth had also witnessed another stepmother die in childbirth, while being harassed by her husband – who then almost condemned her with his recklessness. She was wary, determined not to trust again.

In Queen Mary's reign, Elizabeth was once again suspected of being part of a plot. Mary believed her part of Wyatt's rebellion, a rebellion led by men including the poet Thomas Wyatt against Mary. and Elizabeth was taken to the Tower. Again, she would admit nothing. She was released back to Hatfield House and there lived quietly, careful not to attract attention. She was at Hatfield when she was told her sister had died and she was queen, and she held her first Council of State in the Great Hall at Hatfield.

After Elizabeth, Hatfield was used very little by the monarchs, and James I gave it to Robert Cecil – Elizabeth's former minster, who became right-hand man to James as well. Cecil tore down a large part of the palace and built a new Hatfield House with the bricks. He was celebrated for discovering the Gunpowder Plot in 1605, but he died in 1612 of cancer – as well as overwork at the hands of Elizabeth and then James – and was buried at Hatfield.

Hillsborough Castle

Hillsborough Castle has witnessed some of the most important moments of Irish and British history and diplomacy.

Hillsborough Castle

Hillsborough Castle is in fact more of a country home than a castle or palace. Commissioned in the late eighteenth century by the Marquess of Downshire, Wills Hill, to replace the previous 'Fort' in the middle of his family's extensive estate, which had been their home for decades, it was built in the Georgian style. The founder of the family's fortunes, Moyses Hill, a landless second son, joined the army to seek his fortune in Ireland fighting with the Earl of Essex. In 1603, with the defeat of the Irish, Moyses Hill bought some 5,000 acres of land around Hillsborough and within 50 years, the family had become one of the most prominent landowners in Ireland.

Situated in County Down, the centre of the Hill's family estate, it was intended to demonstrate the power and influence of the family. Wills Hill held the post of Secretary of State for the Colonies from 1768 to 1772 and during that time hosted Benjamin Franklin at Hillsborough. According to popular myth they got on so badly that it persuaded Franklin to redouble his support for the colonists in the American War of Independence. Hill was created the 1st Marquess of Downshire in 1789 and generations of marquesses of Downshire used the castle as a base for their diplomatic and political machinations, as well as hosting lavish marriage celebrations, parties and events.

Hillsborough Castle has witnessed some of the most important moments of Irish and British history and diplomacy. The estate was sold to the British government in the early 1920s, and it became the official residence of the governor of Northern Ireland from 1924. It was extensively rebuilt in 1934 following a major fire attributed locally to arson by the IRA, or otherwise to a lighted cigarette dropped by an estate worker tasked with lowering the flag to mark the funeral of the German President Hindenburg.

Wills Hill (left) and
Benjamin Franklin (right)

When direct rule was reinstated in 1972, the castle became the official residence of the Secretary of State for Northern Ireland, and it was a pivotal location in the negotiations between the various parties. Mo Mowlam, credited as a prime mover in the achievement of the Good Friday Agreement, served as Secretary of State of Northern Ireland from 1997 to 1999. When she died in 2005 her ashes were scattered in the grounds of Hillsborough Castle. It served as a venue for many more important meetings afterwards including Queen Elizabeth II's historic meeting with the Irish President Mary McAleese in 2005.

The gardens, extending to 100 acres, were established when the castle was built, so have many mature trees, specimens and exotic plants. Successive occupiers have added to them and in the 1940s the wife of the second governor created the Granville Rose Garden – she was Lady Rose Bowes-Lyon, the elder sister of Queen Elizabeth, the Queen Mother. In March 1946, Princess Elizabeth made her first visit alone to Northern Ireland to launch HMS *Eagle*, staying at Hillsborough Castle with her aunt and uncle.

The castle has seen American presidents – Benjamin Franklin visited in 1771 and George W. Bush in 2003 – as well as hosting Queen Elizabeth II and Prince Philip as part of the Golden Jubilee tour of 2002, and King Charles III in 2022. As the official residence of the British government and the monarchy in Northern Ireland for many years, Hillsborough Castle is is now run by Historic Royal Palaces and is open to the public.

Kew Palace

Queen Charlotte was an enthusiastic naturalist and the gardens associated with Kew owe much to her interest in cataloguing and drawing the plants and flowers growing there.

Kew Palace

Kew Palace is the smallest of the royal palaces. It was built in 1631 for Samuel Fortrey, a wealthy London silk merchant descended from Huguenot refugees. The house that became known as the 'Dutch House' was built in then-fashionable red brick and laid in Flemish bond with bricks arranged with sides and ends alternating. In 1728, George II and Queen Caroline were first attracted to it as a lodging for their three eldest daughters, and it subsequently became a weekend retreat for the royal family to enjoy a more private domestic life away from their public duties in London. As a boy, the future George III lived there and when he succeeded to the throne in 1760 and married Charlotte of Mecklenburg-Strelitz, they spent much of their early married life at Kew.

Queen Charlotte was an enthusiastic naturalist and the gardens associated with Kew owe much to her interest in cataloguing and drawing the plants and flowers growing there. The gardens also included a menagerie with exotic birds and animals including a pair of black swans, buffaloes and the first kangaroos to arrive in England. As the family grew (George and Charlotte had 15 children), Kew became too small and they moved to Windsor, although the family still looked upon it as their 'country' house, and George III bought the 'Dutch House' in 1781 after years of leasing the estate. Near to the palace, Queen Charlotte commissioned herself the building that became known as Queen Charlotte's Cottage, a thatched 'cottage' in rustic style, very fashionable at the time.

In 1788, King George III's temper was growing increasingly wild. He had long been irritable and irascible, garrulous and controlling. Now, he was becoming sick with stomach problems and delirious, and he seemed to have lost control of his perceptions. He started talking endlessly and fell into mania. Panicked about what might happen, the government demanded he be kept quiet and the household sent the king to Kew Palace to be cured. There, doctors tried different tactics to treat the increasingly distressed king. Arsenic-laden powders were applied to his skin to make it burn and blister; leeches were used; he was starved and plunged into freezing water; and given emetics to force him to vomit. The idea was that the king's illness would be drawn out of his body. None of these so-called remedies worked.

The queen, desperate, turned to Dr Francis Willis, who had a private asylum in Lincolnshire. He came to Kew, and applied a straitjacket and a gag to the king. The jacket was kept on until the monarch was calm, and once he was deemed calm, he was allowed to see his family. If he fell into mania again, the doctor forced him into the jacket. The king was devastated and distressed. But by 1789, he was much recovered (although perhaps that would have happened naturally). His son had wished to be Regent, and although a Bill was introduced, the king was deemed well. But in 1810, the king fell ill again, after the death of his favourite daughter, Amelia. The Prince of Wales became Prince Regent in 1811 and celebrated with a giant party at Carlton House. By the end of 1811, the king was deemed entirely insane and sent to Windsor Castle. It was there that Queen Charlotte's body was brought in 1818, even though she died in her bedroom at Kew Palace. The courtyard was covered with straw so that the king would not hear the procession and understand that his wife had died.

When he came to the throne, George IV thought of demolishing Kew, but did not. His successor William IV commissioned plans to bring it back into use but this did not happen. He offered it as accommodation for Victoire, Duchess of Kent and her daughter, the future Queen Victoria, but the duchess turned it down as 'an old house quite unfit for the princess and me to occupy'. In 1898, Queen Victoria gave the buildings that remained of the palace at Kew to Kew Gardens, and it is now run by Historic Royal Palaces.

Stirling Castle

It was under the Stuart kings that Stirling became the place we know today. James IV kept a great court there, with a magical furnace for alchemy, and James V extended and added to the palace.

Stirling Castle

When Prince James, the future James VI of Scotland, was born at Edinburgh Castle, he was quickly transferred to Stirling Castle, where he was christened and brought up in a lavish nursery. Stirling was thought to have healthier air than Edinburgh and it was also secure. Mary herself had lived at Stirling Castle as an infant. She rode to visit her son regularly, and it was on the way back from one of these meetings in 1567 that she was met on the road by James Hepburn, Earl of Bothwell, with many soldiers. He told her there was rioting in Edinburgh, he must come with her – and she was outnumbered. He took her to Dunbar Castle, and there sexually assaulted her. He did so to force her to marry him, for she would have refused otherwise. Mary accused him and he admitted it – but there was nothing to be done. Mary had to marry Bothwell – she guessed that the lords of Scotland all agreed (indeed, Bothwell had taken a bond from them) and so she would have little defence if she attempted to refuse. Also, women who had been sexually assaulted were expected to marry their attacker. Mary believed she was pregnant, and indeed she was. It was a miserable wedding at Holyrood, with the bride wearing black for her dead husband, Lord Darnley. Bothwell's refusal to share power set the lords and Mary's half-brother against him, and Mary was soon in captivity, never to see her son again.

Stirling Castle dates back to before Roman times; it was probably occupied as a hill fort and used by the kings of Scotland from at least the early twelfth century. In the thirteenth century, the English invaded Scotland and took Stirling Castle, but it was recaptured after Robert the Bruce triumphed at the Battle of Bannockburn. Robert II and Robert III built the earliest remaining sections of the castle, but it was under the Stuart kings that Stirling became the place we know today. James IV kept a great court there, with a magical furnace for alchemy, and James V extended and added to the palace. After his death, the infant Mary, Queen of Scots lived at the castle with her mother, Mary of Guise, and was crowned there in 1543. Stirling was deemed safe from her enemies and Henry VIII, who wanted to seize her – and at the age of five she was sent to the French court.

Mary's son James was christened at a lavish ceremony in Stirling Castle, at a cost of £12,000 – the equivalent of millions today – a tax paid by the towns and Church of Scotland. The grand masque saw an artificial castle erected and besieged by Highlanders, a giant firework display, and a sumptuous banquet served by nymphs and satyrs on a moving table; there were also various *mise en scènes*, including a child descending from a globe in the centre of the room. All of James's attendants were dressed in gold and silver tissue, and ambassadors came from Europe. When Mary, Queen of Scots was forced to abdicate in 1567, James became a king at the age of one. He spent much of his early life at Stirling, essentially imprisoned and never to see his mother again. When he was declared adult ruler in 1579, he barely visited Stirling – until his wife, Anne of Denmark, wished to have her child there, and so the castle had to be repaired. Prince Henry's christening was even more lavish than his father's had been. The fish course was served on a full-sized boat, with mermaids and shooting cannons.

Stirling was used little after James VI and his family moved to England; it became a prison for the high-born in the seventeenth century and was run as a barracks, before it was later opened as a museum.

Linlithgow Palace

The palace is one of the great ruined palaces in Europe; the voices of those who have gone before haunt its walls.

Linlithgow Palace

Mary, Queen of Scots was born at Linlithgow Palace in 1542. Her father fell into despair at the thought of his heir being a girl (two sons had died as babies); already sick and dispirited after a massive loss to the English, he died six days after her birth, at the age of 30. His baby daughter was queen. It was fortunate that the English ambassador deemed her 'likely to live'. Mary of Guise and her infant daughter remained at Linlithgow, before being escorted by armed guard to Stirling. They were terrified that enemies among the lords of Scotland or English spies would seize her.

Linlithgow Palace stands on a low hill above a small loch, 15 miles west of Edinburgh. The site was first occupied in Roman times. It was a manor house dating back to at least the twelfth century and has been a royal residence since the reign of David I (1124–53), who also founded the nearby town. Because of its strategic location it became a base for the English during Edward I's military campaign against the Scots. In 1302, the English built a fort enclosing the manor designed by James of St George, the architect of Edward's Welsh castles. In 1313 it was retaken for the Scots, aided by a local hay supplier who blocked the gates to allow the army in.

In 1424, James I started rebuilding Linlithgow as a palace rather than a castle in grand style after he was freed from English captivity – where he had been part of the English court and fought with the English army. Over the following century the palace was extended by successive Scottish monarchs. It became used by the royals as a rest stop on the way between Edinburgh and Stirling. Among the many visitors to the palace over these years were the exiled King Henry VI of England and Perkin Warbeck, the pretender to the English throne, in 1495.

In 1503, the palace was given to Mary Tudor, wife of James IV and sister of Henry VIII, when she came to be married. James V was born and baptised at Linlithgow but later went to Stirling Castle. The building continued under James V and, in particular, he added the elaborate courtyard fountain, a three-tiered structure decorated with emblematic carvings, now the oldest surviving of its kind in Britain. James was also responsible for the imposing entrance portal built around 1533, which included engravings of the four European orders of chivalry. Linlithgow was intended to be a Renaissance palace and one of the few built as such in Britain.

Under Mary, Queen of Scots, the palace was perhaps at its most vivid and populated, for she visited often before she was deposed. Her son James VI spent little time there and then moved to England in 1603. Decay followed with the collapse of the whole North Wing in 1607. King James authorised its rebuilding and this was to be completed ready for the king's visit in 1622, but he never came. Thereafter, the only reigning monarch to stay at the palace was his son Charles I in 1633. The palace declined further and its last distinguished visitor was Bonnie Prince Charlie who visited during his time in Scotland, leading the Jacobite rebellion, but did not stay – it was said the fountain ran with wine for his arrival. On the night of 31 January 1746 the English army of the Duke of Cumberland contrived to destroy the roof and much of the building by accidentally burning it. The palace fell into ruin and is one of the great ruined palaces in Europe; the voices of those who have gone before haunt its walls.

Marlborough House

Top Sarah, Duchess of Marlborough
Bottom Queen Anne

The letters of Queen Anne to the glamorous, charismatic Sarah, Duchess of Marlborough are passionate and devoted ... They corresponded under the names Mrs Morley and Mrs Freeman – as if they were equals.

Marlborough House

'If I write whole volumes, I could never express how much I love you,' wrote Queen Anne to Sarah, Duchess of Marlborough. The letters from the queen to the glamorous, charismatic Duchess of Marlborough are passionate and devoted. The two became friendly as girls at court, when Anne was rather overlooked and excluded; Sarah, however, noticed her and won her heart. They corresponded under the names Mrs Morley and Mrs Freeman – as if they were equals. But they were not: Sarah was brilliant and intelligent, but her efforts were directed towards gaining power over Anne. As the latter was the younger daughter of the king, few thought she would come to much, but Sarah saw otherwise.

Sarah fell in love with John Churchill at the age of 15 and married him but she stayed at court, keeping her marriage secret to remain a maid of honour, until she became pregnant. When Anne became queen, she made Sarah Mistress of the Robes and gave her other honours, including Keeper of the Privy Purse. After Anne, Sarah was the most powerful woman in the country – and hugely rich.

Sarah had control over every part of Anne's life. However, as Anne grew into her role as queen, she became increasingly weary of her friend's demands, as Sarah pushed her advantage too hard, demanding that Anne do as she advised at every turn. Also, Anne wanted emotional support from her friend, for her difficulties as queen, her frequent illnesses, and her devastating series of miscarriages and infant deaths, but Sarah was often away from court. So the duchess suggested that her own relation, Abigail Hill, a poor cousin, should come to court in 1704 and the queen became increasingly drawn to Abigail's gentle nature – a contrast to Sarah's. Anne felt that Sarah was insufficiently kind to her after her husband's death in 1708 and was also angered by her refusal to wear mourning clothes. In 1710, Anne made it clear to Sarah that their relationship was at an end – and she and her husband would lose their offices. Abigail became Keeper of the Privy Purse, and Sarah retired to Marlborough House. After her husband died, she received many offers of marriage, including from men who had tried to undermine her at court.

In 1708, Queen Anne had granted Sarah and John a lease, at a low rent, of a large portion of land that had been occupied partly by the pheasantry of St James's Palace. They built a huge house there, designed by Sir Christopher Wren – although Sarah argued with him part way through and oversaw the rest of the construction herself. The Duke of Marlborough bought cheap bricks in Holland while on campaign and had them sent back to England. The house was completed in 1711 – in time for Sarah to retire to it after she fell from favour. She died at Marlborough House at the grand age of 84, after a life of great energy and determination.

The successive dukes lived in Marlborough House until 1817, when it was bought as a wedding present for Princess Charlotte of Wales, daughter of the Prince Regent, future George IV. After her tragic death in childbirth at Claremont House, her husband Prince Leopold lived at the house and took a keen interest in the upbringing of his niece, Princess Victoria, at Kensington Palace, but he left in 1831 to become king of the Belgians. Queen Adelaide, widow of William IV, lived there, and the National Art Training School – the future Royal College of Art – was housed there during Victoria's reign. When Edward, Prince of Wales and son of Victoria, married Princess Alexandra, they took the house as their London home and lived there until he became king, when they moved to Buckingham Palace. After the death of the king, Queen Alexandra lived at the house for the rest of her life, as did Queen Mary after the death of George V. Queen Mary installed a rotating summer house and Queen Alexandra added a cemetery for her favourite pets, mostly dogs but also rabbits. King George V had loved his dog Caesar, who trotted behind the horses in his funeral procession, and the queen gave the dog an elaborate headstone to 'Our beloved Caesar who was the King's Faithful and Constant Companion until Death and My Greatest Comforter in my Loneliness and Sorrow for Four Years after'.

Queen Elizabeth, the Queen Mother hoped to live in the house after the death of George VI, but Marlborough House was deemed too neglected and the renovations too costly, so she moved to Clarence House. In 1959, the queen gave Marlborough House to the Commonwealth and it became the headquarters of the Commonwealth Secretariat in 1965.

CÆSAR

Osborne House

Throughout her reign, Victoria returned again and again to her favourite place, even after the death of her beloved Albert ... It was also the place where Victoria wanted to spend the last years of her life.

Osborne House

Built in the middle of the nineteenth century to a design led by Prince Albert, Osborne House was intended to be an escape for the royal family from the bustle of modern London life and the royal court. Queen Victoria had visited the Isle of Wight as a child and stayed close to the Osborne site, so she remembered it well. When she had the opportunity to purchase the estate, she did not hesitate, although it did not take long before she and Albert decided the existing three-storey building was not big enough for their purposes.

Construction of the new Osborne House took from 1845 to 1851. Prince Albert was deeply involved in the layout and design of both the house and the gardens, and found the project a welcome diversion from his other royal duties, as well as an opportunity to display his own talents. Always somewhat irked by his wife's pre-eminence, he was delighted to be able to contribute to the design of their perfect holiday home.

As well as the house and its extensive gardens, Osborne had access to a private beach. During the many summer holidays that the royal family spent on the Isle of Wight, this was a perfect place for the monarch and her loved ones to relax, away from prying eyes. However, Victoria had her own bathing machine, which would take her out into the waters.

As well as having found a secluded spot, and enjoying the quiet it afforded them, Victoria and the rest of her family saw the benefits of demonstrating to the people their happiness and the perfection of their home life. They posed for artists and photographers, and the subsequent images were circulated around the world. The modern image of Victoria and her extended family owes much to their time at Osborne.

During the many decades in which Osborne House hosted the royal family, many

upgrades and changes were made to the design and structure of both the main house and the various outbuildings. Victoria and Albert built a Swiss-style chalet in the grounds, with everything made to three-quarter scale, as a playhouse for their children. The 'Swiss Cottage' became a learning tool, as the royal offspring were taught how to grow vegetables and cook them, under the supervision of both their parents and the staff.

Victoria and Albert built a Swiss-style chalet in the grounds, with everything made to three-quarter scale, as a playhouse for their children. The 'Swiss Cottage' became a learning tool.

Throughout her reign, Victoria returned again and again to her favourite place, even after the death of her beloved Albert. It was the site of the first public telephone call in the country, when Alexander Bell came to demonstrate his new invention to the queen (she said it sounded 'rather faint', but was impressed enough to want to purchase her own set of the equipment). Osborne was also where Victoria wanted to spend the last years of her life – she died there in January 1901, attended by many of her children and grandchildren.

Osborne was dear to Victoria's heart, and she wanted it to remain in the hands of her children, but King Edward VII donated Osborne House to the nation on the day of his coronation. Part of the estate soon became a home for junior naval cadets prior to them heading to Dartmouth, including future kings of England – both Edward VIII and George VI were enrolled there. It was also the location of the confusion over the theft of a postal order, which led to the famous play *The Winslow Boy*, by Terence Rattigan.

Osborne House was also used as a place where injured soldiers – mostly officers – could recuperate from their wounds, and during the First World War both Robert Graves and A.A. Milne were sent there. The glorious grounds and ample accommodation were considered the perfect location for injured and recovering servicemen, and the house was used in this manner until the end of the twentieth century.

Now open to the public, it remains one of the most striking of the royal palaces. Lavish and spectacular, yes, but also designed as a family home, it gives us an insight into the desires and demands of royals who knew they were entering an age of public attention unlike any that had been seen before.

Lochleven Castle

Mary was then taken to 'a great gloomy tower in Lochleven. She was there shut up, within an iron gate, in such a miserable condition, that no poor criminal could be treated worse'.

Lochleven Castle

Mary, Queen of Scots had visited Lochleven Castle, on an island in Loch Leven, a few times as queen, including once to recover after a fall while riding. In June 1567, she was dragged back there a prisoner. She had initially been imprisoned in Edinburgh, but the anger of the ordinary people on her behalf was too great, and so she was taken off to far away Loch Leven, where she could not reach her supporters and the crowds could not demand her freedom. She was pregnant and very ill after she arrived, following her painful defeat by the lords led by her half-brother, James Stuart, who – although the illegitimate son of James V – was bent on winning power. He was working with English spies and aimed to be the Regent for the baby Prince James. In July, Mary suffered the painful miscarriage of the twins she had conceived with her cruel husband, Lord Bothwell, and while she was recovering, she was visited by lords who forced her, at pain of death, to abdicate. As Mary's secretary later recorded, the Lords Lindsay, Ruthven and Melville arrived in her room, along with two notaries, while she was in bed; they sent away her servants, so she had no witnesses, and told her they brought letters for her to sign to abdicate her position as queen. She refused to sign but was made aware that they could simply throw her into the lake or put her in prison where no one would ever see her again. Lindsay specifically told her that he advised her to sign, for if she did not, she would compel them to cut her throat, however unwilling they might be. She had seen the lords stab David Rizzio, her private secretary, in front of her, so she knew they were ruthless. Mary continued to be courageous and demanded to speak in front of Parliament to answer the charges put against her, but Lindsay said he had no instructions. As Claude Nau, a secretary of Mary's, said: '[they] compelled her Majesty by threats and present violence to sign these instruments, which they caused to be read by the said notaries. When they asked her what she thought of the matter, she answered several times that she did not consent to the contents of these instruments, that she had signed them in direct opposition to her intention and will, and that they had been extorted from her by force and constraint.' Mary was hopeful that they would be overturned, as she had been forced to sign them, but it was not the case. Her reign was over; her son was declared king, and her half-brother, who had always plotted for power, was Regent. Mary was then taken to 'a great gloomy tower in Lochleven. She was there shut up, within an iron gate, in such a miserable condition, that no poor criminal could be treated worse'. She was forbidden ink and paper, so she had no way of getting letters to her supporters. Her enemies had done all they could to remove power and agency from Mary – but even though she was heartsick, ill, betrayed and weakened, she was still determined. It was the beginning of her efforts to escape Lochleven – and, she hoped, win back her throne.

Dating back to the fourteenth century, Lochleven Castle was guarded by the Douglas family, the relations of James Stuart – her half-brother who hated her – and Mary worked hard to win over young George Douglas, who agreed to try to help her escape. She nearly managed to escape dressed as a laundress – with her lady-in-waiting pretending to be her, back at the castle – but the boatman recognised her (some said because her hands were too white). She attempted to scale the walls, but she did not succeed; finally, after nearly a year in Lochleven, when the entire castle was enjoying a party, young Willie Douglas helped her to escape after stealing the keys while the guard was in a drunken stupor. She escaped dressed as a servant to be met by horsemen and rushed to Niddry Castle. She gathered her loyal nobles, but there were threats everywhere and she ended up riding to sanctuary in Dundrennan Abbey. There she made a fateful decision. Rather than fleeing to France, where the king would have offered her refuge, or gathering support and attempting to regain her throne, she decided to cross to England and rely on the kindness of Elizabeth I. Once there, she expected to be escorted to visit the queen at Greenwich Palace or Hampton Court, but instead she was immediately placed under house arrest – the beginning of nearly 20 years of imprisonment in England.

Lochleven Castle passed between families but by the early eighteenth century only a picturesque tower remained in the gardens and it fell into ruins in the nineteenth century, before being given to the government in 1939.

Lochleven Castle
SCOTLAND
Edinburgh
Glasgow
Niddry Castle
Dundrennan Abbey
ENGLAND

Richmond Palace

It was Elizabeth I who most loved the palace and its proximity to Richmond Park for hunting stags.

Richmond Palace

In 1603, Queen Elizabeth I was dying at Richmond Palace at the age of 69. After nearly 45 years on the throne of England, the girl who had been constantly excluded as a child, almost executed by her brother and then her sister, and always seen as a bastard by Europe and many in England, had become one of the greatest monarchs in history. She had created brilliant propaganda about the Virgin Queen, married to the nation. After all, her people saw that the marriages of her sister Mary I and her cousin Mary, Queen of Scots had been catastrophic, with their husbands demanding power and undermining their wives in every way. But now the queen was dying without an heir. She had been suffering from failing health, and had also been struggling with melancholic thoughts after the death of friends and, some said, the execution of her cousin, Mary, Queen of Scots, many years before. The nearest to the throne, and her expected heir, was James VI of Scotland, son of Mary herself. But the queen would not name her successor. She was determined to remain seated on a cushion as she prepared to pass. Her minister Robert Cecil told her she should go to bed, but she refused, telling him that 'must is not a word to use to princes'. However, as she sickened she was forced to lie down, but she still refused to assign her heir. Finally, she held up her hand. It was deemed as a signal to accept James as her heir, and so consent was given – and the Tudor period was over.

Richmond Palace had been the site of the betrothal of Princess Margaret, sister of Henry VIII, to James IV of Scotland. They were the great-grandparents of James VI – the beginning of the Stuart line, which had provided Elizabeth I's great rival in the shape of Mary, Queen of Scots. And now, in James I, they would continue the monarchy.

There had been a manor house on the site of Richmond Palace since the twelfth century, if not before, as Sheen Manor House. Edward I took occupation of the house in the thirteenth century. When Queen Isabella, known as the She-Wolf, was the Regent for her son Edward III, she was in possession of Sheen and spent much time there. Richard II loved the palace, where he lived with his wife, Anne of Bohemia, but when she died of plague, he was heartbroken and ordered it to be demolished. It was rebuilt by Henry V and Henry VI, but then in 1497, in the reign of Henry VII, there was a huge fire that destroyed much of the palace, and the king and queen and their family had to run for their lives, almost killed by flying debris. Henry VII rebuilt it and named it Richmond Palace, for his title, Earl of Richmond. Henry VIII used the palace, and his daughter Mary spent part of her honeymoon with Philip of Spain there. But it was Elizabeth who most loved the palace and its proximity to Richmond Park for hunting stags. After Elizabeth, the palace was little used: James I preferred Whitehall, and when Oliver Cromwell took over the country the Protectorate sold off the palace as building materials. It was never rebuilt but some parts still remain, including the Gate House.

In 1603, Queen Elizabeth I was dying at Richmond Palace at the age of 69. The girl who had been almost executed by her brother and then her sister ... had become one of the greatest monarchs in history.

St James's Palace

St James's Palace was built by Henry VIII on the site of a lepers' hospital dedicated to St James. It was a 'back-up' palace to the greatly significant Whitehall Palace, used by the king to escape court life.

St James's Palace

In 1688, Mary of Modena was due to give birth at St James's Palace. She had fallen pregnant after 10 years of marriage and the court was rife with suspicion that she had a 'fake bump' and had invented the pregnancy. Her husband, James II, had had two daughters with his first wife, Anne Hyde, but a son would displace them both. James and his wife were distrusted as Catholics, whereas the two daughters – Mary, married to William of Orange, and her younger sister Anne – were Protestant. The thought of James's child continuing the dynasty was anathema to the court, so when Mary of Modena gave birth to a healthy baby boy, James Francis Edward Stuart, the rumour mill went wild that she had faked the birth and a spare infant had been smuggled in, in a 'warming pan' – a seventeenth-century hot-water bottle. It was exceedingly unlikely, but no one wanted James II's child to inherit and so there were maps drawn of the palace, decreeing that it would have been easy enough to take a child in a pan through the corridors. James proffered the testimony of around 70 witnesses to the birth, but they were mocked and lampooned in the press.

The 'fake baby' was the beginning of the end for James II and Mary of Modena. In the following year, they were deposed for Mary and William of Orange. The latter invaded, and when he arrived leading aristocrats joined his army. James's army was greater, but he was too nervous to attack and instead attempted to flee, throwing the Great Seal into the Thames. Parliament declared that these actions meant that James had essentially abdicated, and William should take the throne. Mary and her son, the prince fled to France; William took James prisoner but didn't want an extra king on his hands so let him escape to France. It was supposed to be

a joint monarchy but really William was the king and, significantly, Mary, who was the daughter of the former king, was crowned with a consort's crown. James Francis Edward Stuart spent the rest of his life trying to win back the throne, and his son, Charles Edward Stuart, known as Bonnie Prince Charlie, staged an invasion of England from Scotland in the mid-eighteenth century, but he was quickly pushed back.

James II had been born at St James's Palace. After his father, Charles I, went to war with the Parliamentarians and was captured, he was taken back there and kept under house arrest with his siblings, Henry, Elizabeth and Henrietta. When the terms for Charles I's continued rule could not be agreed, Parliament pondered whether they should use the teenage James as their king. Charles told him to escape.

On 20 April 1648, James played hide-and-seek with his siblings in the gardens of St James's Palace. In the bushes, he met a Royalist agent, Joseph Bampfield, and they planned to meet later. That night, James wished his sister goodbye and hurried down the stairs – but he fell and the crash made him think he had been detected. He went back to his room, where he realised that no one had noticed, so he dashed down the stairs, into the garden and into a waiting carriage with Bampfield. The spy took him to another house, dressed him as a woman and took him to a fishing boat in the Thames, in order to escape to Holland. James was free, but his escape meant that his father would be watched more closely than ever. Charles had already been trying to escape his own prison at Carisbrooke Castle, but he had got stuck in the bars of his window. He was determined, and bought nitric acid to melt down the bars and saws to chop them out. But the brilliant escape of his son James meant that he had no chance, and he would be executed within the year.

Over 100 years after the 'warming pan' baby, the Prince of Wales, the future George IV, was waiting in St James's Palace to meet his new fiancée, Princess Caroline of Brunswick. He had been the most debauched Prince of Wales in history, carousing with mistresses and spending wildly. The seven sons of George III were, in the words of the Duke of Wellington, 'damn'd millstones around the neck of the country' and George was the worst of the bunch. His father George III compelled him to marry to clear his shocking debts but he had little interest, declaring all German princesses the same. He was actually already, secretly, married to the beautiful Maria Fitzherbert, a commoner and a Catholic. It was breaking the terms of the Royal Marriages Act: a law made by George III, decreeing that royals needed his permission to marry. A popular cartoon by James Gillray, 'The Lover's Dream', showed George in bed cuddling a pillow, while his mistresses and his drinking and gambling friends, as well as a cure for venereal disease, lurked by the bed. The king's envoy, Lord Malmesbury, was dispatched abroad to see George's proposed bride, Caroline, and reported that Princess Caroline had 'fine eyes'

When Mary of Modena gave birth to a healthy baby boy, James Francis Edward Stuart, the rumour mill went wild that she had faked the birth and a spare infant had been smuggled in, in a 'warming pan'.

but 'figure not graceful' and 'tolerable teeth but going'. He worried she was too much of a gossip and too 'curious'. Caroline was married by proxy and sent over to meet her cousin for the first time. After a long sea journey, she arrived in London and St James's Palace. She kneeled to the prince, who raised her – and he then rushed away, declaring: 'I am not well, pray get me a glass of brandy.' He was horrified and went straight to the queen.

George had essentially deserted Caroline within weeks ... He spent the rest of his life trying to divorce her. When he was told at Windsor Castle, 'Sire, your greatest enemy is dead,' he replied, 'Is she really?'

Caroline was equally unimpressed. She declared loudly that George was very fat and 'nothing so handsome as his portrait'. The prince had cruelly given Caroline his mistress, Lady Jersey, as a lady-in-waiting, and Lady Jersey missed no opportunity to tyrannise her.

The doomed marriage went ahead at St James's Palace. The prince was hopelessly drunk, and clasped the hands of his brother and said, 'Tell Mrs Fitzherbert I shall never forget her.' On the wedding night, he collapsed with his head in the grate, drunk. He was repulsed by Caroline's looks and smell, and fascinated by Lady Jersey. George had essentially deserted Caroline within weeks and separated from her in the following year. He spent the rest of his life trying to divorce her. When he was told at Windsor Castle, 'Sire, your greatest enemy is dead,' he replied, 'Is she really?' His greatest enemy was Napoleon, of course, who had died in July 1821 on St Helena, but he was still obsessed by divorcing his wife. They had somehow managed to conceive a child, and Princess Charlotte was born at the beginning of 1796. The only legitimate granddaughter of George III, the entire future of the dynasty rested on her. When she died in childbirth, George and his brothers were plunged into the chaos of having no heir.

One of the brothers, the Duke of Cumberland, was caught in a shocking scandal in 1810. In the early hours of the morning, the duke shouted out to his valet that he had been murdered, after being hit on the head in bed with his sword. The duke's other valet, Joseph Sellis, was later found in his room with his throat slit. The newspapers went wild that there had been jealousies between the three, and a book later accused the duke of killing Sellis himself to prevent him from revealing details about homosexual lovers. The duke sued for libel. Paying visitors crowded into the palace to investigate the crime scene and solve the mystery but the murderer was never apprehended.

St James's Palace was built of red brick by Henry VIII on the site of a lepers' hospital dedicated to St James. It was a 'back-up' palace to the greatly significant Whitehall Palace, used by the king to escape court life and sometimes to lodge royal guests. The clock over the gatehouse is inscribed with the initials HA for Henry and Anne. After Whitehall was burned down at the end of the seventeenth century, it became greatly more significant and the centre of administration for the monarchy, as it is today. George III found it cramped and uncomfortable, and purchased Buckingham House to be a more spacious alternative. Buckingham Palace displaced St James's as the monarch's principal residence in the eighteenth century. St James's is the senior royal palace and the official title of the court is the Court of St James's. When Charles III became king, the proclamation of the new sovereign was issued from St James's Palace and the Accession Council took place there.

Royals have frequently kept their mistresses at St James's. Both George I and George II gave them rooms there, and William IV lived there with his illegitimate children by Dorothea Jordan. He banished her and told their offspring they had to choose between their parents – and he kept those who chose him in St James's Palace with him, much to the despair of the mother of the future Queen Victoria, who thought it immoral. Poor Queen Caroline, formidable wife of George II, suffered a terrible death because of a hernia; it should have been pushed back in and sewn up, but instead the doctors cut it off, and subjected her to repeated, painful, useless operations, without opium to relieve her suffering. The poor queen's bowel burst just over a week after she was first taken ill and then she died three days later, in dreadful pain.

Queen Victoria was married to Prince Albert at St James's Palace, after she proposed to him – she had to do so, as she was queen. The wedding was rather shocking to many onlookers, for Victoria and her bridesmaids wore white.

Queen Victoria was married to Prince Albert at St James's Palace, after she proposed to him – she had to do so, as she was queen. The wedding was rather shocking to many onlookers, for Victoria and her bridesmaids

wore white. She and her ministers planned a white wedding to emphasise Victoria's youth and purity – unlike her debauched uncles George IV, William IV and their brothers. Victoria's dress was made of fine Spitalfields silk satin and Honiton lace. She herself said: 'I wore a white satin dress, with a deep flounce of Honiton lace, an imitation of an old design. My jewels were my Turkish diamond necklace & earrings & dear Albert's beautiful sapphire brooch.' Few brides wore white for their weddings, and would instead wear any colour, often muted tones – royal brides had sometimes worn silver, a material of great expense. The queen was determined to show herself in her open carriage on the way to St James's, not looking too draped in luxuries. The old days of George IV and jewels and excessive spending on fashion were over; she aimed to appeal to a new middle-class sensibility about getting and spending. Onlookers thought she and her bridesmaids looked like peasants in the too-simple gowns, but the die was cast, and as soon as Victoria was seen in her white wedding dress the trend caught on, and all of Victorian England was marrying in white. The portraits of Victoria's mother at the wedding at St James's show her looking less than thrilled: she had planned to gain power over her daughter throughout her childhood, aiming to be Regent. But William IV had thwarted her efforts by holding on to life until Victoria turned 18. However, even after Victoria became queen, it had been unseemly for her to live in Buckingham Palace without an escort, so her mother lived with her, and Victoria blamed her for disputes within the household. By marrying, Victoria could finally ensure her mother would have to move out. The new queen was delighted by her wedding, and had no idea she was sparking a juggernaut of a bridal trend.

Victoria said: 'I wore a white satin dress, with a deep flounce of Honiton lace, an imitation of an old design. My jewels were my Turkish diamond necklace & earrings & dear Albert's beautiful sapphire brooch.'

In the twentieth century, St James's Palace was often used for diplomatic meetings, including the 1931 conference on Indian independence. On 12 June 1941 the United Kingdom, Australia, New Zealand, Canada, South Africa and General de Gaulle of France, as well as the exiled governments of Belgium, Czechoslovakia, Luxembourg, the Netherlands, Greece, Norway, Poland and Yugoslavia signed the Declaration of St James's Palace, which was the first of six treaties instituting the United Nations.

Eltham Palace

Further expansions were seen under Richard II, Henry IV and Edward IV, who created the great hall, still surviving, which once hosted a Christmas feast for 2,000 people.

Eltham Palace

Eltham Palace is a stunning art deco mansion in south-east London. The first record of habitation in the area is in the Domesday Book, when the manor of Eltham was owned by Bishop Odo of Bayeux, who was William the Conqueror's half-brother. By the last years of the thirteenth century, it had passed to the Bishop of Durham, Antony Bek, who enclosed the current site with a stone wall inside the existing moat.

Bek handed the manor to Edward II in the early fourteenth century, and he oversaw more expansion and repairs; his son, known as John of Eltham, was born there in 1316. Edward III also spent much time there and oversaw yet more repairs and alterations, and the palace remained a key part of the English court for centuries. Further expansions were seen under Richard II, Henry IV and Edward IV, who created the great hall, still surviving, which once hosted a Christmas feast for 2,000 people.

Henry VIII spent much of his childhood at Eltham, and once again the estate saw considerable investment and occupation. But towards the end of his life, he began to prefer Hampton Court and Greenwich Palace. Elizabeth I barely visited Eltham and the place fell into disrepair; during the Civil War, it was sold to Colonel Nathaniel Rich, who destroyed much of the structure and sold the lead from the roof. For many years afterwards, the land was farmed and the remaining buildings were rented out, and the great hall used largely as a barn.

In the early nineteenth century some effort was made to bring the complex back into a more usable state. New buildings were constructed, including a relatively lavish new villa, and parts of the largely filled-in moat were converted into gardens, both decorative and kitchen. Some work was done to stabilise the great hall, which from time to time was

used as a tennis court and party venue. Just before the First World War, the governmental Office of Works replaced the roof, which for years had been at risk of collapse.

In the early 1930s the palace was leased from the Crown by Stephen and Virginia Courtauld, a wealthy couple who had made millions from the textile industry. They commissioned the architects Seely and Paget to restore the palace and turn it into a luxurious residence. The result was a stunning art deco masterpiece that combined large parts of the medieval architecture with modern design elements. It served as a place to display their wide-ranging art collection, and they twice hosted a visit from Queen Mary – probably the first major royal to visit since Charles I – and also revamped the extensive and beautiful gardens.

The Courtaulds installed many modern conveniences into their new building, including underfloor heating, a centralised vacuum-cleaner system and a telephone exchange.

During most of the Second World War they remained in residence, although the structure sustained some damage from both incendiary and regular bombs at various points. Towards the end of the war, the threat of bombing became too much for the Courtaulds, and they gave up the lease and handed Eltham Palace over to the army, which used it as a training base until 1992. Some years before that, the army had scaled back their operations and the site had been opened to the public. After English Heritage took over the entire site, it worked to refurbish the house, outbuildings and gardens to reflect their 1930s heyday.

Windsor Castle

Windsor Castle has seen many royals, many secrets, many battles. But it is most associated with Elizabeth II, the queen who loved it most ... for whom it was both wartime home and retreat from London.

Windsor Castle

In the Second World War, princesses Elizabeth and Margaret were evacuated to Windsor Castle. Along with them, the king sent the most precious of the Crown Jewels to be hidden in the grounds – in a biscuit tin. The most valuable jewels from the Imperial State Crown worn by the monarch after their coronation – the Black Prince's Ruby and St Edward's Sapphire – were removed, stored in the tin and then placed in a special hiding place under a trapdoor. The jewels had survived Oliver Cromwell seizing and dismantling the crown and the king wished them to survive in the event of an invasion. The details were so secret that very few people knew about them, not even Princess Elizabeth.

On 2 March 1882, Queen Victoria was travelling from Windsor Station to the castle, cheered by boys from Eton College. She then heard an explosion, thought it was an engine, but realised she had been shot at. The schoolboys used umbrellas to capture the shooter, 28-year-old Roderick Maclean, who was later found not guilty but insane. It was the eighth attempt to shoot the monarch, which began with a first attempt at Buckingham Palace. Victoria was sanguine about what Elizabeth Barrett called 'this strange mania for Queen-shooting'. 'It is worth being shot at to see how much one is loved,' Victoria said.

Home to 39 monarchs over the years, and now stretching to a thousand rooms and nearly 500,000 square feet of space, Windsor Castle is the oldest inhabited castle in the world, and has seen great history play out inside and outside its walls. It was where Elizabeth I waited out the plague, Charles I was imprisoned before he was executed, Victoria mourned Albert, and the sky over Windsor – and Eton and for miles around – flamed in November 1992 when the castle was ablaze. The castle was such an icon of royalty that its name was chosen by the royal family in 1917 to replace Saxe-Coburg-Gotha.

When William the Conqueror invaded England in 1066, he singled out Windsor as having key strategic importance, due to its position near the Thames, a day's march from London, as protection for the western side of the capital. Windsor Forest had long been valued by kings as a hunting ground, but William laid the foundations for Windsor to be a royal stronghold. The outer walls now are as they were when they were built, as is the mound under the Round Table and the Upper Ward – the location of the private royal apartments since the fourteenth century.

Henry VIII used the grounds for perfecting his athletic prowess – shooting, dancing, wrestling (usually they let him win) – and built himself a tennis court at the castle.

Windsor Castle was one of a series of castles built for fortification reasons by William the Conqueror, but it is the only one that remains. It was not, however, used as a royal palace until the reign of Henry I, William's fourth son, who came to the throne in 1100. In 1120, the White Ship – the ship carrying Henry's son and heir, William, and his court – sank off the coast of France, after hitting a rock (the crew and the passengers were drunk). Henry I's wife, Matilda, had died two years earlier and he married Adeliza of Louvain, holding the wedding at Windsor Castle itself. The castle came to be increasingly occupied by the successive monarchs. When King John was threatened by the revolt of the barons, he took position at Windsor Castle and met them to dicsuss terms at nearby Runnymede where he signed the Magna Carta in 1215.

Edward III rebuilt the castle, adding not only large and beautiful apartments for the king and court, but also the great hall for his new order of chivalry, the Knights of the Garter in the 1360s.

The Tudor period saw a great moment for the castle. When Henry VII came to the throne, he staged a giant feast for the Order of the Garter, and this continued for his son – some of Henry VIII's dinners were so grand that there simply was not room for everybody. Henry VIII used the grounds for perfecting his athletic prowess – shooting, dancing, wrestling (usually they let him win) – and built himself a tennis court at the castle; he was also frequently there for his beloved hunting. It was, moreover, useful to him as a place of isolation – Catherine of Aragon was confined to Windsor when Henry was discussing divorcing her. He was fond of Windsor Castle, and St George's Chapel was finally finished in his reign; when he died he was buried there, alongside his third wife, Jane Seymour. The vault where Jane Seymour was buried was meant to be temporary. Henry had great and fabulous plans for his tomb, some of them borrowed from the plans of his former minister, Cardinal Wolsey (who, of course, was buried with little ceremony after falling from grace). Henry planned a huge bronze effigy of himself on top of a high sarcophagus surrounded by 10 pillars, bearing statues of the Apostles, and an altar at the end, supported by yet more pillars and decorated with effigies of angels. The whole thing would have been encased in a chapel made of black marble and bronze, in which he expected daily masses to be said for him. The tomb would have taken up a lot of space in St George's Chapel. Henry made elaborate plans, had his cast made when he was still alive and even took Wolsey's sarcophagus to save money. All looked set for a magnificent tomb.

Henry's son, Edward VI, thought the castle unappealing and rather too Catholic in its ceremonies. When he took refuge there during the unrest and rebellions in 1549, he was exceedingly unhappy with it, declaring: 'I am in a prison, here are no galleries, nor no gardens to walk in.' However, he did commission some building work, using stone that had been part of abbeys across the country. Despite the time he spent at Windsor, Edward VI did not complete his father's tomb. He asked in his will for it to be completed, but Mary I (perhaps fairly, after the way Henry had treated her mother) did nothing.

Elizabeth I was very fond of Windsor Castle, and rebuilt and extended it. In the summer of 1560, two years after she came to the throne, she spent time nearly every day with her dear friend Robert Dudley. She had appointed him Master of the Horse, the only man officially allowed to touch the queen. He had left his wife, Amy Robsart, at home in Oxfordshire. On 8 September, Amy sent her servants to a nearby fair – and when they returned, she was at the bottom of the stairs, dead of a broken neck. She was also found with head wounds. Scandal broke out, and

Henry had great and fabulous plans for his tomb, some of them borrowed from the plans of his former minister, Cardinal Wolsey (who, of course, was buried with little ceremony after falling from grace).

even though Dudley spent the equivalent of over a million on his wife's funeral, people said he had killed her in order to marry Elizabeth. Amy had been sick with an abscess of her breast, but she was some way from dying naturally. If Elizabeth had hoped to marry Dudley – a complicated question, as even though she was devoted to him, he was a commoner and the son of a traitor, and people expected her to marry a prince – now that there was such a scandal around his wife's death, she would never be able to, and she had to separate herself to a degree from him. The death seems unlikely to have been an accident, due to the wounds, and suicide would have been seen by Amy as a terrible sin. The evidence suggests that ambassadors knew about the death even before it happened and it makes the most sense that, if it was not an accident, the killers were Dudley's enemies –

or rogue agents attempting to act on their behalf, foreign powers or possibly those at home, who wanted to lessen his influence over the queen.

Elizabeth later suggested Dudley as an ideal husband for Mary, Queen of Scots – and recommended that the couple should live at court with her. Mary was offended by the suggestion of a commoner and a traitor's son – not to mention the taint of a strange death of one wife – and refused. Instead she rushed to marry Henry, Lord Darnley, a man with a claim to the English throne, which infuriated Elizabeth. Darnley's vanity and aggression would be the beginning of the end for Mary.

Elizabeth was at Windsor when the plague broke out in June 1563, five years after she had come to the throne. By August, a thousand Londoners were dying every day. Elizabeth and her court fled to Windsor and the queen erected gallows in the town square to discourage anyone from coming too close. She even refused to allow goods to be imported from London, in case the plague could be spread by the carts. Henry VIII had seen the castle as a place of pleasure. For Elizabeth, whose position was much more insecure than her father's had been – the politicians around her were constantly in fear of attempts on her life from anything from rogue courtiers to poisoned gloves – Windsor was a refuge, a place where she went in case of attack or siege. When the trial of Mary, Queen of Scots was taking place for treason against her, she took refuge in Windsor in case of rebellion. She bought 10 new cannons and even spent money on extending the palace – quite something for the famously parsimonious Elizabeth. She built the Long Gallery in order to have a spot where she could take walks in bad weather. However, the extensions were never quite enough, and the castle was often crowded, as dramatised in a play requested by Elizabeth herself, William Shakespeare's *The Merry Wives of Windsor*. Henry's tomb, which would have been the most magnificent in the Chapel, had stalled. Elizabeth looked at plans and had the component items moved to Windsor – but no progress was made. James I disinterred his mother, Mary, Queen of Scots, from Peterborough Cathedral, where she had been buried after her execution, and built her an elaborate grave in Westminster Abbey, but he had no interest in doing the same for Henry (historic attacker of Scotland), whose tomb languished untouched and with no marker in St George's Chapel.

The merriment continued with James I, who enjoyed the hunting at Windsor and used it as a drinking venue. His son, Charles I, extended the castle, bought paintings for the collection and commissioned a grand gold service for the altar of St George's Chapel – but he was creating his own prison.

In the Civil War, Windsor Castle was taken over by Parliamentary forces, as it was a key location for protecting London. John Venn, who was later one of the signatories on the death warrant for Charles I, became commander of the castle until 1645. Prince Rupert tried to take the castle in 1642 but failed, although he managed to take the town of Windsor. After his attempt, the soldiers made more effort to fortify the castle, including creating ditches and fortified walls. Some soldiers were billeted in local inns – John Quigly's inn in Windsor had 50 soldiers staying there (he later claimed for a huge £46 in expenses for the cost of them) and Widow Ffookes's inn was accommodating 25 men – but the majority stayed in the castle, and they needed supplies. The surrounding areas were expected to pay for the fortifications and to give the garrison money, food and usable items, especially beds. They were usually taken from houses but in some cases local people had to take their belongings for 'donation' to the castle. One Widow Dorothea Colins, late wife of John Colins, of Ripplesmere Hundred, in March 1645 had 'two bedds, two bolsters, two payre of sheets and two coverlitts' as well as a kettle taken from her house, the total value of which was £3 10s. When the soldiers finally left Windsor, there were 113 feather beds left behind, all of them 'relieved' from the local population. Some of the local villages were also expected to pay taxes to the Royalist forces.

It wasn't just beds and horses taken from the population; the forces also raided items from the castle, particularly the chapel, where the organ was destroyed, and the books and valuables seized. The parts of Henry VIII's tomb, which had been languishing at Windsor, were sold off, and the bronze effigy was melted down and sold.

From 1643, the castle was used to imprison Royalists – Edward VI's complaint that the castle was a prison came true. Finally, in 1647, it held its greatest prisoner of all, when King Charles I was captured. He had escaped from the siege of Oxford and rushed north in a daring operation, dressed as a servant, and after being taken prisoner, he had escaped again but got stuck in a window on the Isle of Wight. He was held at Windsor Castle briefly after his capture and then again in the final weeks of his reign. The archives still hold his copy of Shakespeare's *First Folio*, inscribed at the front in Latin, 'while I breathe, I hope'. Charles's hope was in vain: he was executed at the beginning of January outside Banqueting House. He was taken back (with his head sewn on his body) to be buried unceremoniously in the vault with Henry VIII, now overlooked and ignored – a location chosen to deter people making a martyr of the dead king.

Under Oliver Cromwell, the Crown Jewels were melted down and the royal palaces fell into disrepair. Windsor Castle had been occupied by 'paupers' and apparently the whole place was a 'wreck'. Charles II, restored to the throne in a blaze of glory in 1660, set about restoring the castle to its former grandeur, with a giant building plan (he also planned to build a grand mausoleum for his father in Hyde Park, but this never came about). He created the lavish state apartments, decorated with wood carvings by Grinling Gibbons and ceiling paintings and murals by Antonio Verrio, and laid out the famous Long Walk from the castle into Windsor Great Park. Charles's plans were cut short by his death at the age of 54.

The successive Stuarts preferred Hampton Court, although Anne, with her eye for garden design, noted the lack of a formal garden in Windsor Castle and commissioned one from Henry Wise, but it was never completed. For Anne, Windsor Castle was the scene of the greatest grief of her reign, when her young son, William, died there just after celebrating his eleventh birthday. George I and also George II cared little for Windsor and the castle fell into disrepair, but then started attracting the first tourists. It was a place for the wealthy visitor, as a little money to the Castle Keeper would ensure that a tourist could peruse some of the treasures, and the first guidebooks to the castle were published in the 1750s.

George III took the throne at the age of 22, in 1760, and Windsor's fortunes were entirely reversed. Unlike those before him, he did not wish to keep Hampton Court as his country residence. He did not initially wish to live at Windsor Castle, but his brother refused to vacate the Ranger's Lodge, so George and Queen Charlotte moved into the long-neglected royal apartments and set about renovating them in Palladian and later Gothic style, at the cost of over £150,000 (around £40 million now). Nicknamed Farmer George, he laid out farms in the ground built two dairies and restored Virginia Water lake. The castle became beautiful and magnificent once more. However, for the daughters of George III, Windsor Castle was a gilded prison. The king had seven sons and six daughters. The former left to set up homes with mistresses and behaved scandalously; George, Prince of Wales, his eldest son, seduced women and spent wildly, and when

Under Oliver Cromwell, the Crown Jewels were melted down and the royal palaces fell into disrepair. Windsor Castle had been occupied by 'paupers' and apparently the whole place was a 'wreck'.

forced to marry, he used all his time trying to rubbish his estranged wife's reputation.

Between them, the many children managed 56 illegitimate offspring and one legitimate child – Charlotte, the daughter of the Prince of Wales, conceived in the brief period when he lived with his wife. The king adored his daughters and did not wish them to leave him. He had his first bouts of poor mental health early in his reign and as they increased with age, he became more determined that his daughters should remain with him. The queen didn't raise the question of marriage for fear of upsetting him; she kept society away as she was trying to hide the king's illness, and so the sisters had little chance of meeting men. The king's illness made him a dysfunctional parent, sometimes angry, sometimes excessively affectionate and even cruel. The princesses seized friendship with any men they could find: Princess Sophia probably began an affair with Thomas Garth, a member of the king's household, and very likely gave birth to his child, a son, who Princess Charlotte feared attempted to secretly befriend her. The king's mental illness grew worse, and he was unpredictable. He was treated brutally in Kew, with restraints and restrictions, which naturally had no effect. Finally, in 1811, the king and queen had to accept that he was unable to govern, and the Prince of Wales became Prince Regent – and the sisters were finally able to marry.

During George III's reign, a use was finally found for Henry VIII's sarcophagus – in 1805, it was taken to St Paul's and used for the body of Lord Nelson, in the aftermath of the Battle of Trafalgar. Nelson's grave, however, remained unmarked.

As Regent, George commanded various building works to Windsor Castle, including building a passage to a new vault in St George's Chapel in 1813. There, the forgotten royal tombs were found and the builders saw that Henry VIII's coffin was smashed. Charles I's coffin was opened, and it was said that George IV's doctor passed the executed king's jawbone around at dinner parties. It was not until the reign of William IV that a marble slab was put on the floor of St George's Chapel to mark the resting place of Henry and Queen Jane Seymour.

George III died in 1815 and the Prince Regent became George IV. He spent the huge sum of £300,000 on renovating and expanding Windsor Castle, rebuilding the private apartments, adding to the royal collections and renovating the exterior in Gothic style for grand balls and receptions. The king himself often lived at Royal Lodge in the grounds and took drives around the park, which was where his niece, the future Queen Victoria, paid him a visit and even saw his royal zoo. As she said: '[I] was driven about the Park and taken to Sandpit Gate where the King had a Menagerie – with wapitis, gazelles, chamois, etc, etc.' On one occasion, the duchess was convinced that the king was kidnapping her daughter, as he whizzed her around the grounds.

When Victoria herself came to the throne at the age of 18 in 1837, she was unconvinced by her uncle's home, declaring it dark and dingy, but although she bought Osborne House and Balmoral Castle as family homes, she used Windsor as a main state residence and did much of her political and dynastic entertaining there.

Victoria met Prince Albert when he visited for her seventeenth birthday; she had been friendly towards him but not bowled over. On a second visit, after she was queen and painfully aware that she had to marry – both for dynastic reasons and because, as a single woman, she had to live with her mother – she saw him quite differently. When he arrived at Windsor Castle, still rather queasy after the long journey, she beheld him standing at the bottom of the stone steps and was utterly charmed. 'It was with some emotion that I beheld Albert,' she wrote. Later, he clasped her hand in the castle corridor before going to bed. Five days later, she summoned him to the Blue Closet and said that 'I thought he must be aware why I wished him to come here, – and that it would make me too happy if he would consent to what I wished (to marry me)'. As Albert wrote to her after the engagement, on a return trip to Germany: 'Since we left, all my thoughts have been with you at Windsor, and that your image fills my whole soul.' After their wedding, in which Victoria broke new ground with her white dress, the pair spent their honeymoon at Windsor. 'There was an immense crowd of people outside the Palace, and which I must say never ceased until we reached Windsor Castle … we came through Eton where all the Boys … cheered and shouted.' Albert wanted six weeks; the queen allowed three days – which were punctuated by entertaining.

Victoria and Albert were fascinated by new advances, and Windsor saw the queen adopt the most important technology of her reign – to take the first journey by train from nearby Slough to Paddington on the Royal Train on 13 June 1842. Victoria loved the Royal Train and travelled widely, although she forbade it from going too fast – there was a belief that going too fast could cause madness.

The Victorian court kept up an exhausting round of entertainments, such as the spectacular visit of Napoleon III of France and Empress Eugénie in 1855. The future Queen Alexandra once surprised the queen by doing an acrobatic move in the castle, and La Peregrina, the most famous pearl in history – later owned by Elizabeth Taylor – was lost in a sofa by the Duchess of Abercorn.

In 1861, Prince Albert fell ill after a tiring journey to try to give a talking-to to his eldest son, Edward, Prince of Wales, and swiftly deteriorated. In the last stages of his illness, the prince asked to be moved to the Blue Room, which was full of light, even in winter. George IV and William IV had also died there.

Victoria was devastated by the death of Albert; a widow at just 42, she kept his room exactly as it had been when he died: the book that she was reading to him before he passed away bears the bookmark at that spot, stored in the archives. When her son, the Prince of Wales, married Princess Alexandra of Denmark, she insisted that they marry in St George's Chapel, so that she could watch the ceremony from a secret royal closet high up – once built by Henry VIII for Catherine of Aragon. The queen spent much of her remaining life at Windsor and Balmoral. At her Golden Jubilee, a giant face of Victoria was apparently created out of fireworks over Home Park, a part of the Great Park the royals had enclosed.

When the queen died in 1901 on the Isle of Wight, she was transported back to Windsor and buried at the Royal Mausoleum in Frogmore.

In 1868, the Emperor of Ethiopia called for help from the British over a border war and wrote to Queen Victoria – but he received no reply. In desperation, he took some Europeans prisoner, and in response the British army staged a full-scale invasion. The emperor released the prisoners and committed suicide, and the British looted and stole all his treasures: jewels, precious objects and books. The Crown Prince Alemayehu was also taken and brought back to England, where he became the ward of Queen Victoria. He begged to be allowed to return to Ethiopia, but his request was denied and he died at the age of 18. He is buried in St George's Chapel, Windsor, and his grave is marked 'when I was a stranger, ye took me in' – although, he'd never asked to be taken in. Ethiopia have repeatedly asked for his remains to be sent back.

As soon as Edward VII came to the throne, he swept through Windsor, throwing away all of his mother's clutter and sentimental possessions, destroying busts of John Brown and disposing of photographs. He put electric lights in all the rooms and installed heating. His son, George V, was particularly fond of living at Windsor and his wife, Queen Mary, commissioned the magical Dolls' House, on show in the castle today. Designed by Lutyens, it is a perfect replica of an elite 1920s home, and even the books on the shelves were actually handwritten by leading authors of the day. When war broke out in 1914, there was suspicion of the king's relatives and a report was made of strange signal lights emitted from the castle (they turned out to be the car lights of a dinner guest as he headed home), so in 1917, the king changed the royal surname from Saxe-Coburg-Gotha to Windsor to sound more British. Not long after they had done so, the law was changed to forbid any other German in Britain from doing the same.

Edward VIII spent little of his short reign at Windsor Castle. He occupied a house in the grounds, Fort Belvedere, where he installed a swimming pool. It was at Fort Belvedere, on 10 December 1936, where he signed the written notifications of his abdication, witnessed by his three younger brothers. His brother, George VI, took the throne and sometimes used the castle. But in the Second World War, the castle came to the fore. The princesses Elizabeth and Margaret were 'evacuated' to what was said to be a secret location – although everybody knew they were in Windsor Castle. There the girls tried to live a normal life, although they heard planes overhead; there were over 70 bombings of the Great Park. The princesses went to bed in 'siren suits', with their suitcases of toys and

supplies packed in case of a bomb alert, when they would flee to the cellars in the castle. The princess gave her first-ever public address from the castle, to evacuated children in 1940, saying that she and Margaret 'feel so much for you' and that, as other youngsters, 'we are trying, too, to bear our own share of the danger and sadness of war'.

American soldiers were billeted at the castle, amusing the princesses by offering them chocolate and saying they had daughters at home just like them. The princesses had an allotment for vegetables in the castle grounds and carried on their education – with Elizabeth visiting nearby Eton for lessons in constitutional history. While living at Windsor Castle, the princesses found many treasures in the basements. They staged pantomimes to raise money for charity, even using George IV's sedan chair, found in the stores. Margaret played Cinderella in 1941 and Elizabeth Aladdin in 1943. Prince Philip, serving in the navy, had been corresponding with Elizabeth since the beginning of the war, after the royal family had paid a visit to Dartmouth Naval College and he had escorted the princess. She fell in love with him then, on the spot, but for Philip, it was when he came to stay with the family, when Elizabeth was 16 and 17, that he became equally set on marriage. When he returned from war, he began courting Elizabeth in earnest.

Queen Mary commissioned the magical Dolls' House, on show in the castle today ... It is a perfect replica of an elite 1920s home, and even the books on the shelves were handwritten by leading authors of the day.

As queen, Elizabeth chose to use Windsor as her weekend retreat and she spent increasing amounts of time there as her reign progressed. She received presidents there, including Barack Obama and Joe Biden, and hosted historic state visits, such as the first state visit from Ireland in 2014.

The queen's silver wedding anniversary fell on 20 November 1992. On the same day, a fire broke out in the private chapel, due to a faulty spotlight setting fire to a curtain, and by 11.30 a.m. it had taken hold in the castle. Furniture was ruined and 115 rooms destroyed. Staff rushed to remove paintings and furnishings (fortunately, many items had already been removed due to rewiring work), forming a human chain to get items out, while 225 firefighters from three counties battled the blaze. The fire flamed above Windsor, to be seen for miles around for 15 hours, until it was finally extinguished at 2.30 in the morning.

The damage was approximately £36.5 million, with around a fifth of the castle destroyed or affected. A huge restoration was planned (and not officially finished until 1997), but a scandal broke out: the newspapers and public protested that it was unfair to ask the taxpayer to pay in a time of recession – the royals should pay themselves.

Four days after the fire broke out, on 24 November, the queen gave a speech referring to 1992 as her *annus horribilis*, not just because of the very public breakdown of her children's marriages, but also due to the devastating fire of her beloved home – and the angry shouts about who was going to pay for the repairs. The queen agreed to open up parts of Buckingham Palace to paying visitors, and the money raised was to help fund the restoration of Windsor Castle.

Edward and Sophie were married at St George's Chapel, and Charles and Camilla at the nearby registry office – there had been plans to hold the wedding at Windsor Castle, but the royals changed their minds, as legally that would allow civil ceremonies to be conducted at Windsor for the next three years – and the reception was held in the state apartments.

During the Covid pandemic, Queen Elizabeth and the Duke of Edinburgh stayed isolated at Windsor with a small staff (called 'HMS *Bubble*'), and she delivered her famous Covid speech from there, declaring: 'We will meet again.' Prince Philip died at Windsor in April 2021 and his funeral was held at St George's Chapel. The picture of the queen mourning alone there, as she was not in a bubble with any other royal family members, is an enduring image of the Covid pandemic. The prime minister offered the queen the opportunity to relax Covid funeral rules for her husband, but she refused, explaining that since the rest of the country must follow the restrictions, there should not be special exceptions for the royals. There was a political scandal when it was discovered that staff at 10 Downing Street had been enjoying drinking parties in the office, including a raucous one on the night before Prince Philip's funeral.

2018 saw the wedding of Prince Harry and Meghan Markle: the world's media descended on Windsor, the streets were packed with well-wishers, and St George's Chapel held celebrities and dignitaries, while the service was beamed around the world. There was a carriage procession through Windsor after the ceremony and then a reception at St George's Hall, followed by a smaller evening reception held at Frogmore House. Harry and Meghan lived near the castle, in Frogmore Cottage, until they left for the United States.

In the grounds of Home Park is Adelaide Cottage, moved to in 2022 by the Prince and Princess of Wales and their three children,

Prince George, Princess Charlotte and Prince Louis after living in London. The family enjoyed the peace and privacy of Windsor. Built for Queen Adelaide in 1831, using materials from the Royal Lodge, Adelaide Cottage was a fashionable cottage which Adelaide used to visit. It has reception rooms and four bedrooms. The ceiling of one bedroom is decorated with ornaments from the yacht HMY *Royal George* including dolphins. Group Captain Peter Townsend, equerry to the King, was given the cottage in 1944 and it was later occupied by the Queen's cousin, Simon Rhodes.

Elizabeth II spent much of the final year of her reign at Windsor Castle, and among her visitors was the actor Tom Cruise; she invited him for tea and apparently allowed him to land his helicopter on the lawn. When one of her corgis, her beloved Candy, died at Balmoral in the summer, the body was sent back to Windsor for burial. Elizabeth II died at Balmoral. After her state funeral at Westminster Abbey, the first to be held in the country since 1965, the queen was taken to Windsor Castle for a committal service and burial at St George's Chapel, Windsor. Near the end of the service, the Imperial State Crown and the Sceptre, which had been positioned on the coffin, were put on the altar. The Lord High Chamberlain broke his wand of office and laid it on the coffin, to symbolise the end of the queen's reign. The queen was later interred in a private service in the King George VI Memorial Chapel, with her father, mother, sister and husband.

Windsor Castle has seen many royals, many secrets, many battles. But it is most associated with Elizabeth II, the queen who loved it most. No one in the future may be as devoted to the castle as Elizabeth, for whom it was both wartime home and retreat from London – and the place where the jewels she later wore as queen were once buried in a biscuit tin.

BATH
OLIVER
BISCUITS

Index

Biographies

About the Author

Professor Kate Williams is a historian, author and broadcaster. She has written 10 historical books, including historical novels such as *Storms of War* and *Edge of the Fall* and biographies on such topics as Elizabeth II, Victoria and most recently on Mary, Queen of Scots. She appears regularly on television and radio, discussing social history, royal history and general politics and culture and has presented various series on Channel 5 and BBC including *Secrets of the Royal Palaces*, *Restoration Home* and *Inside Versailles*. She is CNN's Royal Historian and covers all royal and historical events for television. She studied for her degree and DPhil at Oxford and is now Professor of History at the University of Reading.

About the Illustrator

James Oses is an illustrator. He draws a wide variety of subject matter using dip pens, pots of ink, watercolour, and brushes. Selected clients include *The Financial Times*, English Heritage, Berry Bros. & Rudd, Rotary International, Borough Market, and *The Radio Times*. He has illustrated two other books by author Alex Johnson for Frances Lincoln Publishing: *Rooms of Their Own: Where Great Writers Write* (2022); and a follow up *Studios of Their Own: Where Great Artists Work* (2024).

Author Acknowledgements

While writing this book I have been utterly thrilled every time I have seen a beautiful illustration by James Oses and am very grateful for his artworks, which bring these palaces to life. I would also like to thank my delightful and patient publishers at Quarto, Philip Cooper and Laura Bulbeck, whose wise counsel and incisive thoughts I am very fortunate to have, and also Liz Somers, and everyone who worked on turning my manuscript into this handsome book. This book is dedicated to all those who work and volunteer at these buildings, preserving them for the future.